Compilation published by British Origami Society
Version 2.0, November 2013

Don't Fold Under Pressure is BOS Booklet No. 77

The British Origami Society is a registered charity. Charity Number 293039
www.britishorigami.info

Contents

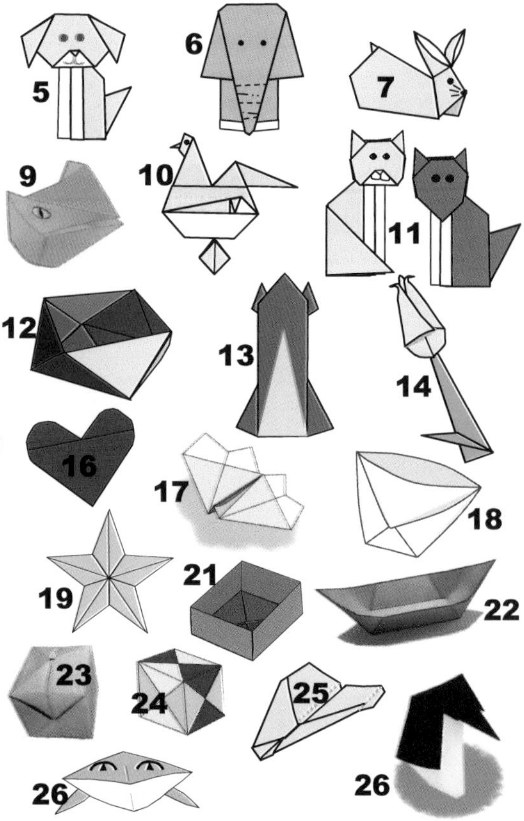

For most of these models, although I have drawn the diagrams, I cannot claim to be the creator. Some of them are 'traditional', but others are more modern. Where known, I have given the name of the person who created the model.

Join the British Origami Society and you will be able to meet with some of the most exciting paper-folders in the world and have access to a unique Library of books and other publications.

You can get origami paper and more from www.britishorigami.info or visit British Origami Society on Facebook.

Contact address if you need any origami help or advice: publications@britishorigami.info

Enjoy your folding!

This book has some of my favourite simple origami models. I hope that you enjoy them too!

David Raynor, 2013

First a word about **Different Kinds of Folds and Symbols....**

A '**valley fold**' is a simple fold that leaves the paper with a 'dip' in it, like this:

It is marked with simple dashes. - - - - - - - - - - - - -

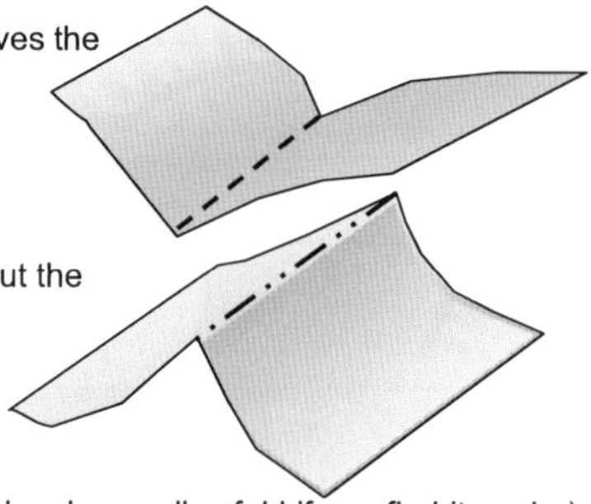

A '**mountain fold**' is the same thing, but the other way up. Like this:

It is marked with dots and dashes:

— · · — · · — · · —

Sometimes you fold and unfold again. This is shown by a double-headed arrow, or a two-way arrow:

(You can often turn the model over and make a valley fold if you find it easier).

This means 'stick up at 90 degrees':

An '**inside reverse fold**' is where the paper is tucked inside the model, like this:

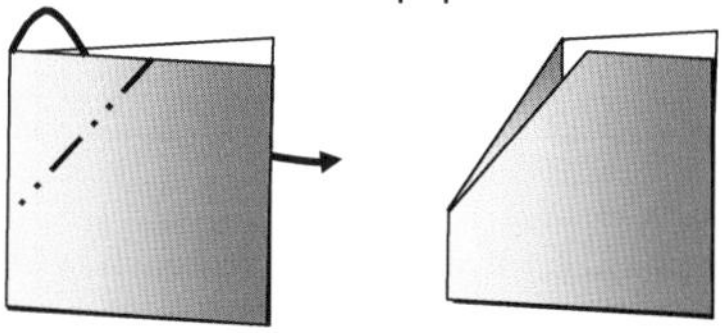

An '**outside reverse fold**' is where the paper is folded back over the outside of the model, like this:

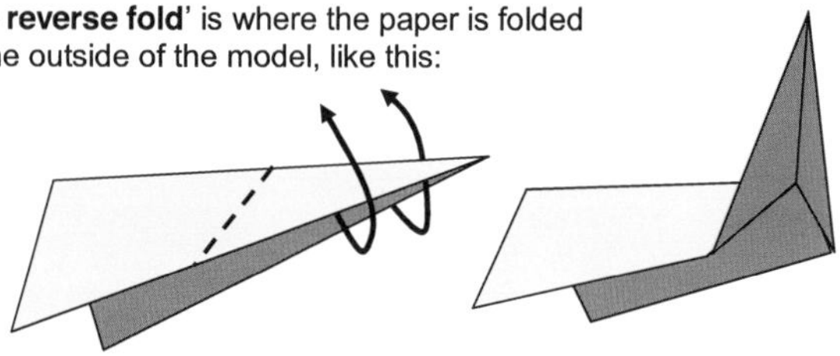

You can combine inside and outside-reverse folds to make pleats. The puppy on page 5 folds the tail inside and then back out again. A pleat is sometimes shown like this:

For beginners, the best tip is to make the folds very sharp, then these reverse folds will be much easier. For most folds in this book, assume that you make them sharp, unless it says not to.
I always say that origami is the best reason in the world not to bite your nails – because you need them to make the folds!

A symbol that you may see often is the 'repeat arrow' -  this is used when the people who draw the diagrams (me) are too lazy to draw everything again! The number of lines going across the arrow are supposed to be the number of times that you repeat everything. It might be accompanied by some numbers, like this:  5-8 to say 'repeat steps 5,6,7,8 three times'. It normally means "repeat on the other side" or on another point. Look at the next picture to make sure.

Another symbol is 'turn over' - 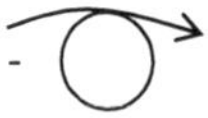 Check the next drawing to see you have done it correctly.

These are most of the folds and symbols that you will need for origami. If you make more complicated models you will meet other ideas like the 'sink' and 'twist folds', but by then you will be good at it. (You can try a sink in the cat's head on page 11 if you feel brave enough!)

I have used a number of different styles when drawing the diagrams in this book. With luck, this will help you get used to diagrams that you find in other books and on the internet.

If you have trouble understanding a move, look at the next picture and it should help to show what the result looks like. It you really don't understand it – then it's my fault, not yours! Let me know if you get stuck by e-mail (contact address is on page 2).

A few more hints and tips that might help you.

Practice! Don't get discouraged if your model doesn't look perfect first time.
You can often use any old paper to practice with – magazines, photocopier paper – you don't have to use expensive "origami paper". You just need to make sure that you have a good square to start with.

To make a square from a rectangle, you just need to fold over a corner at 45°, then fold over the remaining rectange and cut it off, like this:

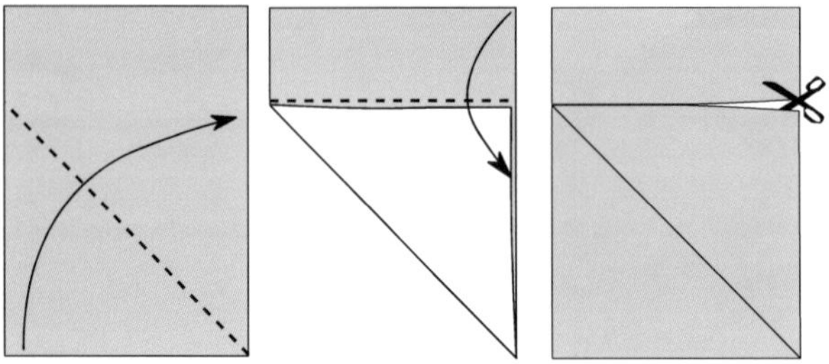

Or lay one sheet over another at 90°, then fold and cut off the overlap.

For some models, paper with a different colour on each side is better – the Penguin model at the back of the book only really looks good in black and white, for example – but for most models it doesn't matter.

When you fold, try to make sure that the paper is smooth all the way along the fold line. Any little dimples or buckling will make it hard to fold an accurate straight line. One tip is to stretch the paper along the line of where you want to make the crease, to make sure that it is as smooth as possible.

For reverse folds, you may be able to open out the model to make it flat where the crease will go. An example is in the Penguin model. The diagram on page 26 shows an outside reverse fold for the head and a couple of folds to pleat the beak in and out. A simple way to do all this is to open out the model with the tummy upwards, then fold the head down, with a small pleat for the beak if you want. Then fold the model in half again. Finally, grab hold of the head and the back of the neck and move the head by brute force until it is pointing the way you want them. Finally squash it all flat to fix it in place. The diagrams for that way of doing it might look like this:

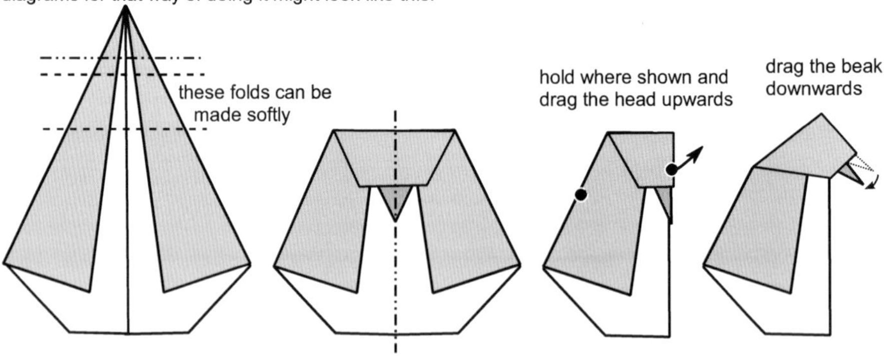

(That is how the author folds it.)

An excellent source of simple models are the 'Page-a-Day' calendars by Margaret Van Sicklen, produced annually by Workman Publishing Inc. Many of the models here were learned by the author from this calendar.

Finally – Have Fun! Laugh at your mistakes and help your friends. It's only a piece of paper!

Puppy

Model inspired by many designers, including Dokuohtei Nakano, Keiji Kitamura and Zsuzsanna Kricskovics

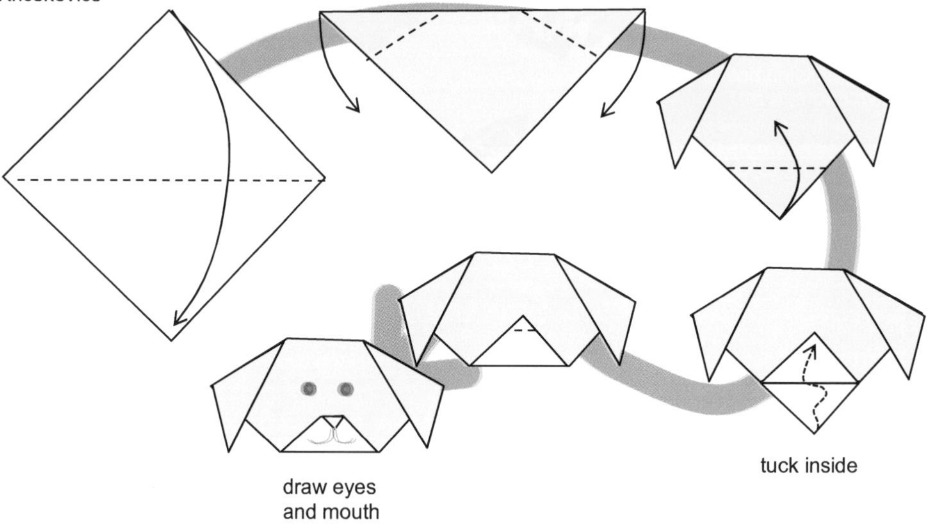

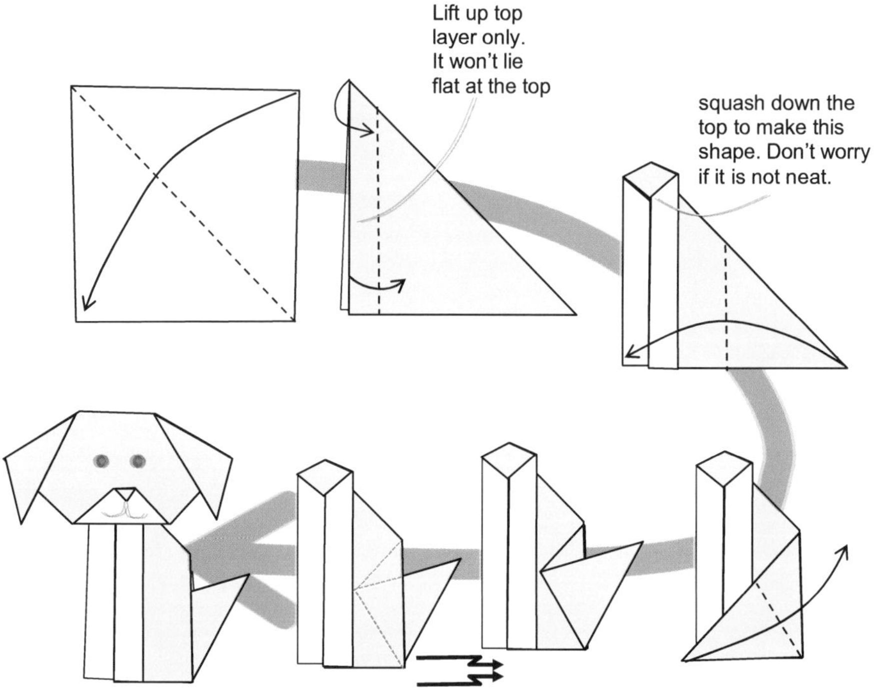

inside-reverse-fold the tail inside and then back out again.

It will look better if the head is made from a smaller square than the body. Say 12cm head, 15cm body.

See also the Cat and Fox on page 11

Elephant

Based on a model by Zsuzsanna Kricskovics

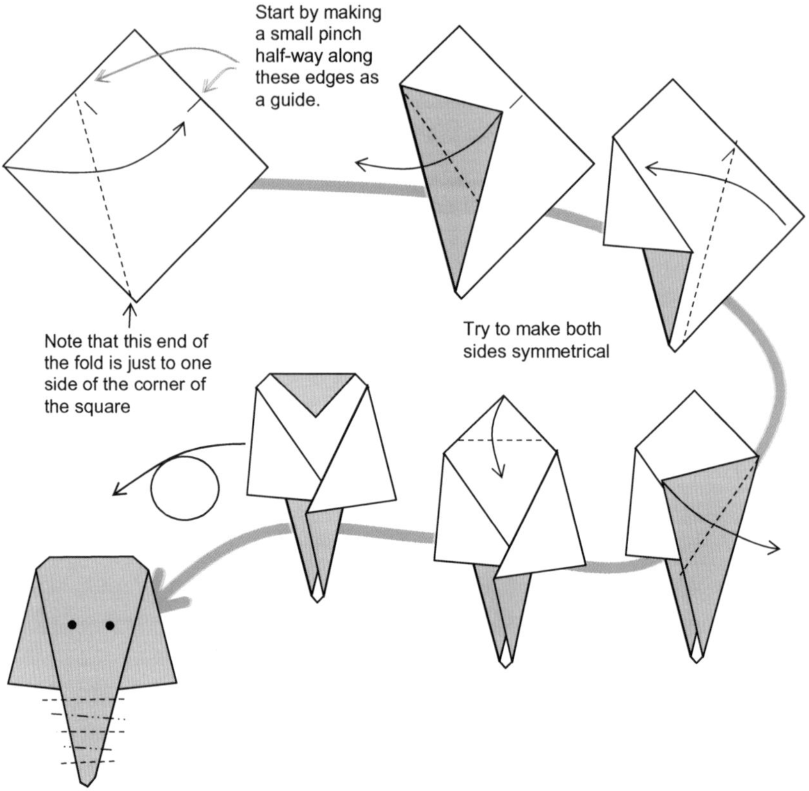

Give it a nice wrinkly nose

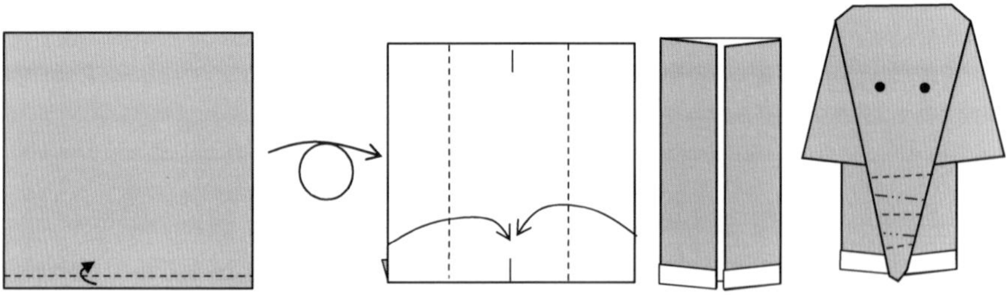

Fold lightly in half to find the middle, then fold the sides in.

Rabbit

Traditional model

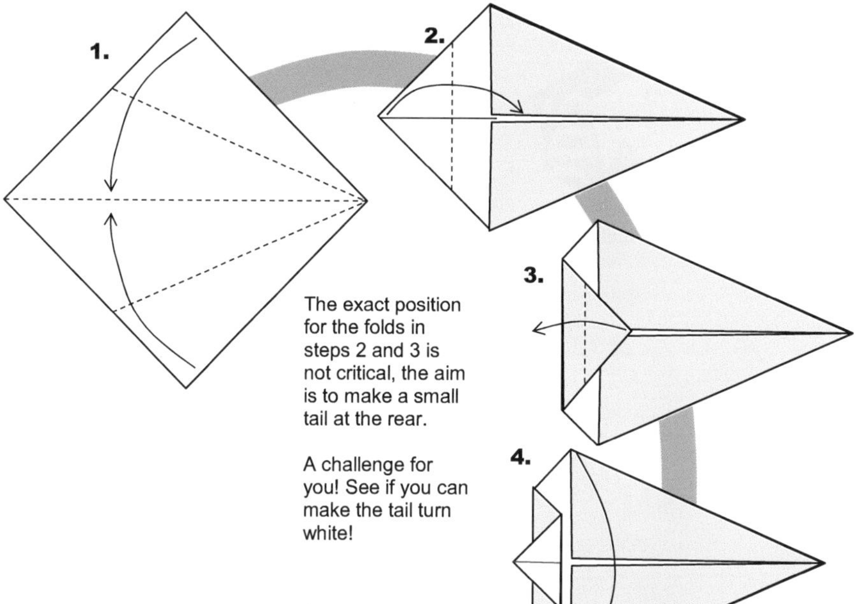

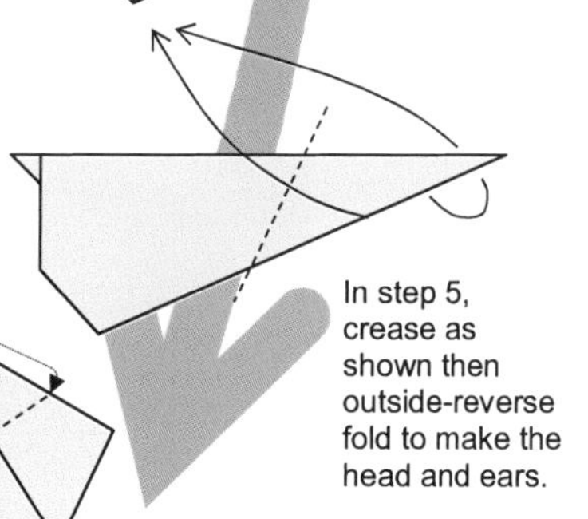

The exact position for the folds in steps 2 and 3 is not critical, the aim is to make a small tail at the rear.

A challenge for you! See if you can make the tail turn white!

In step 5, crease as shown then outside-reverse fold to make the head and ears.

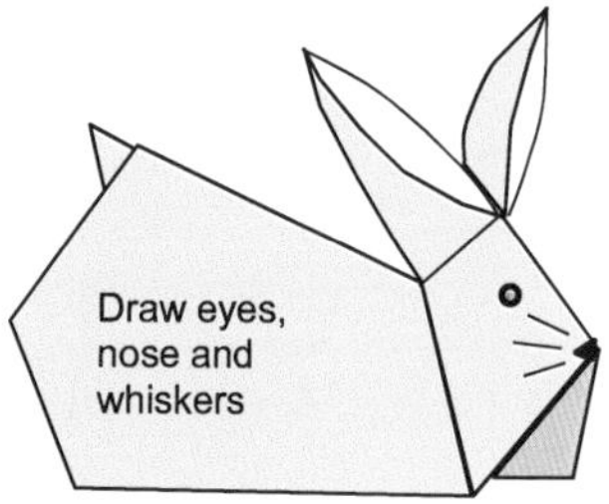

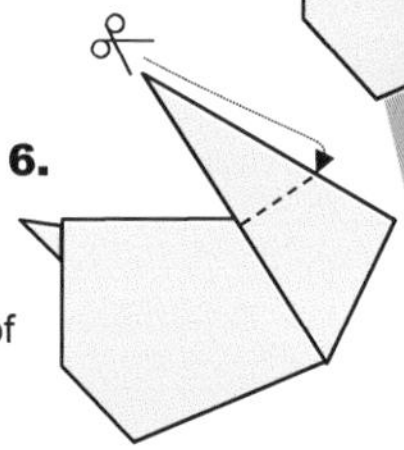

In step 6, cut to separate the ears; just cut to the point shown (about ½ - ¾ of the way down). Then fold them to make them stand apart. Spread the front of the ears open to see the white inside.

It can look really good if you use origami paper that is pink on one side and white on the other. Start with the pink side upwards and make a white rabbit with pink inside the ears!

Preliminary and Waterbomb Bases

A square of paper with valley and mountain folds like this is the starting point for hundreds of different origami models:

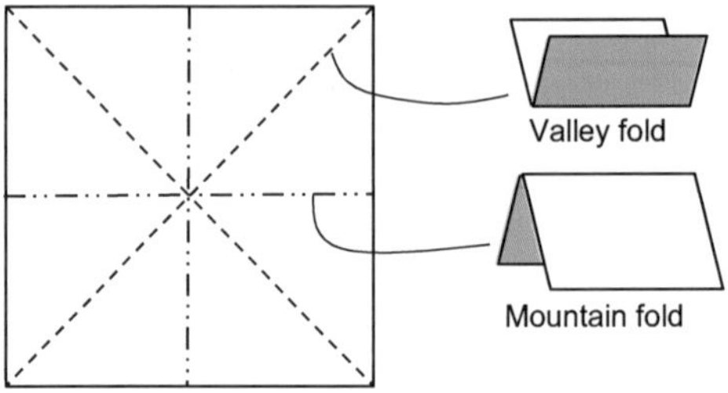

Just fold and unfold the opposite corners together from one side of the paper. Then turn the paper over and fold and unfold the opposite sides together.

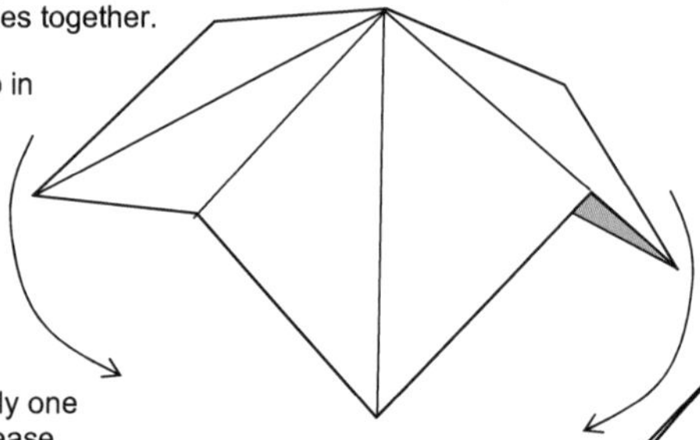

For the **Preliminary base**, press up in the middle from underneath and down in opposite corners and it will collapse in on itself to make a smaller square.
Sometimes this is called the **Square Base**.

It is also possible to make it with only one diagonal fold. That removes the crease from the face of the finished result.
Sometimes you don't want unnecessary creases.

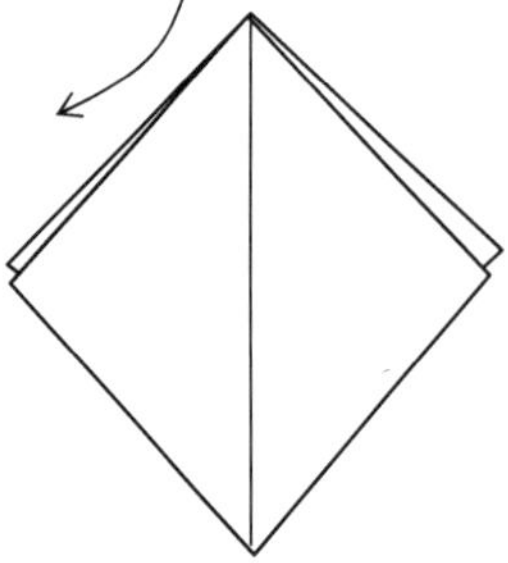

For the **Waterbomb Base** press down in the middle and pinch the corners together.

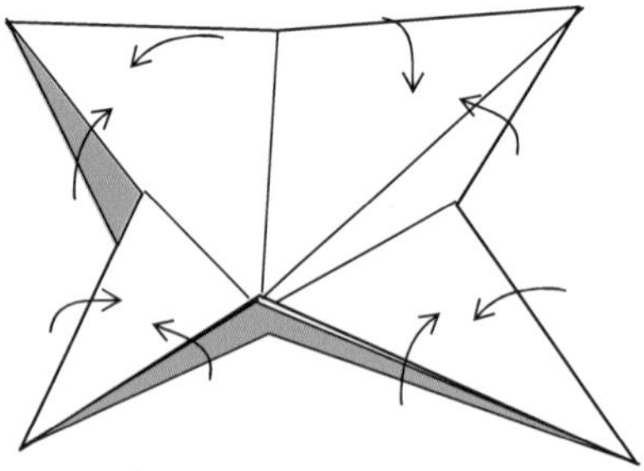

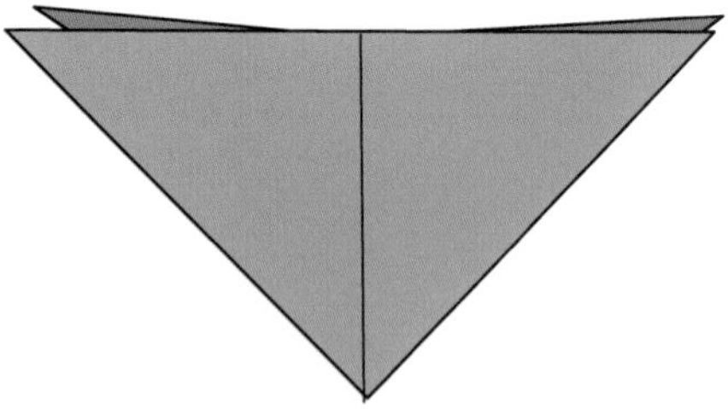

It's a kind of fearsome 4-pointed arrowhead shape.
It is also possible to avoid the central crease for this, if you don't want it in your model. Just miss out one of the 'side-to-side' folds.

Dragon's head

Model from 2002 Page-A-Day Origami Calendar by Margaret Van Sicklen

1.

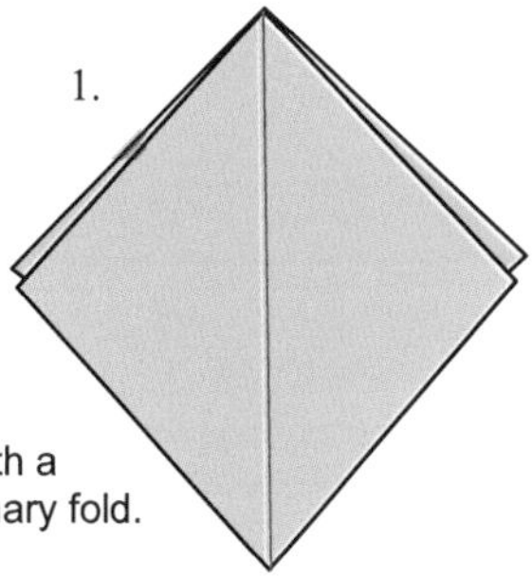

Start with a Preliminary fold.

Open points are at the bottom.

2.

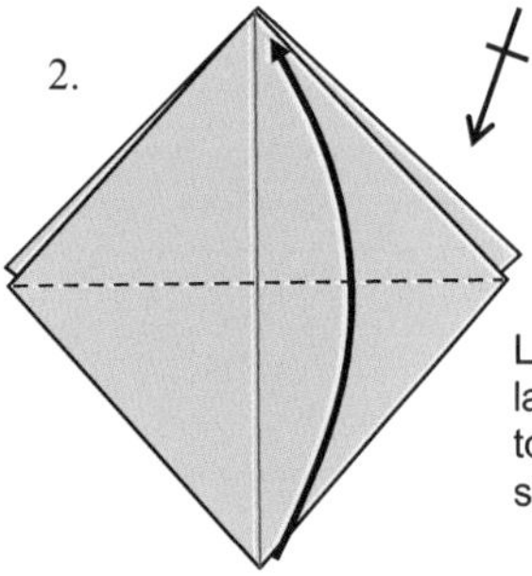

Lift the single layer up to the top, on both sides

3.

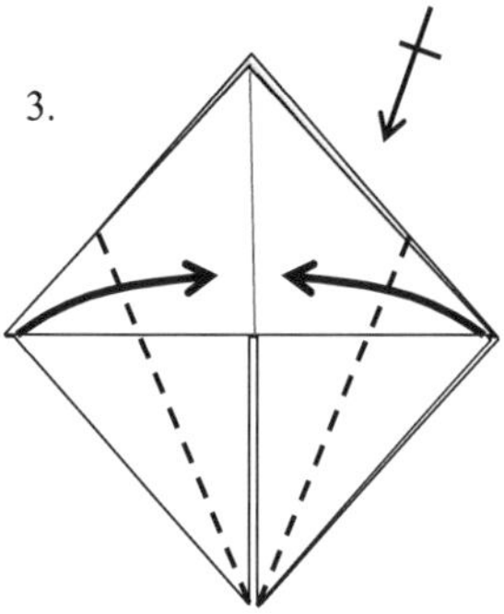

4.

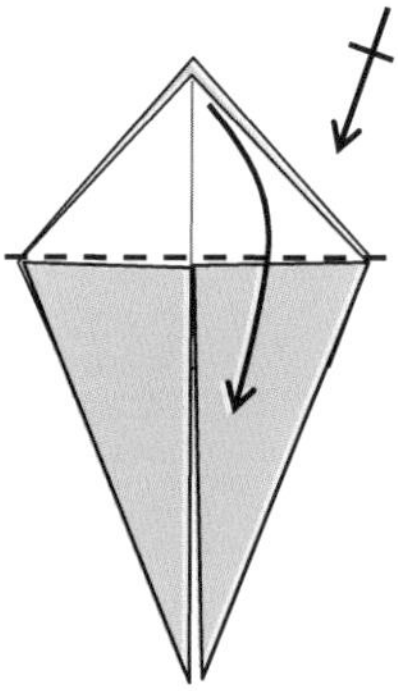

5.

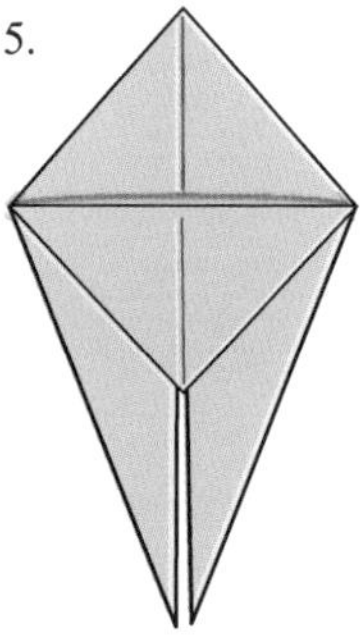

6.

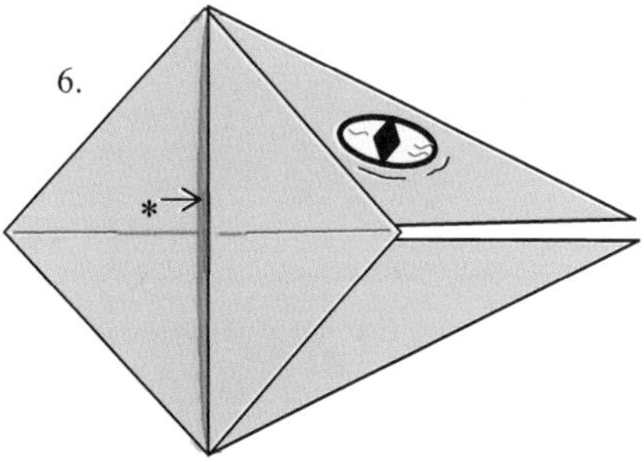

Draw some ferocious dragon eyes on both sides, then put your thumbs inside the pockets (*) on both sides and gently pull your hands apart.

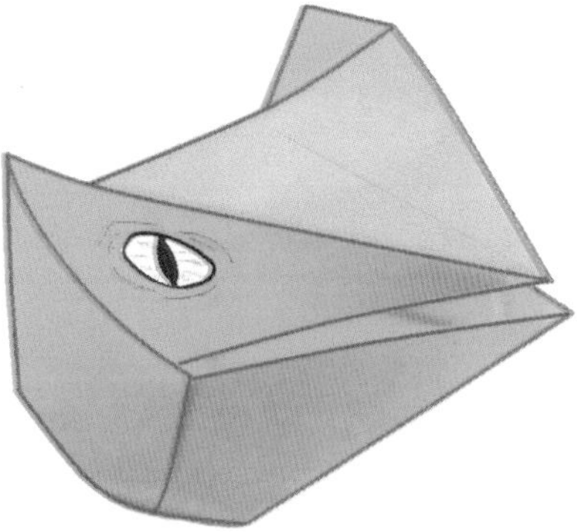

It pops-up, and turns 3D !

Egg-Laying Chicken (it's amazing!)

Model created by Zsuzsanna Kricskovics

1\. Start with a Preliminary fold, colour inside. Open points are at the top.

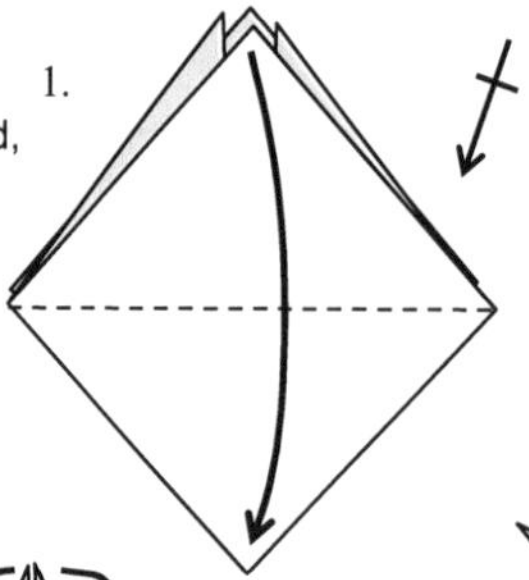

2\. Tuck the edges inside

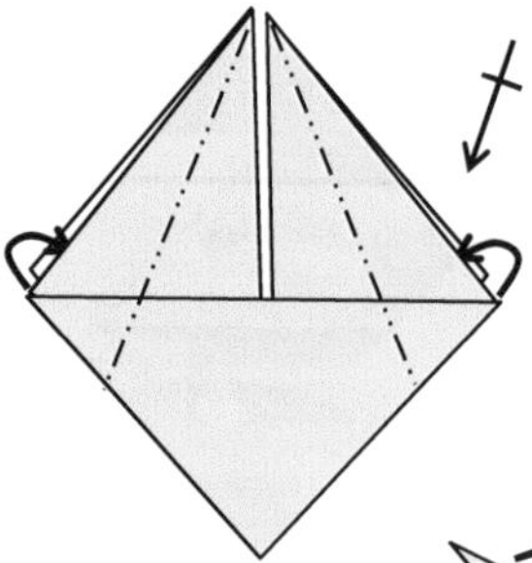

3\. Inside-reverse fold the points. One goes horizontal to make the tail and the other is left pointing up tall, to be the neck.

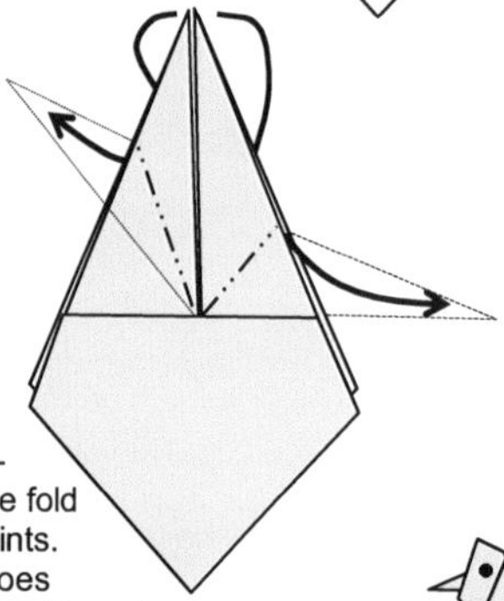

4\. Pleat the single layer on each side to make the wings.

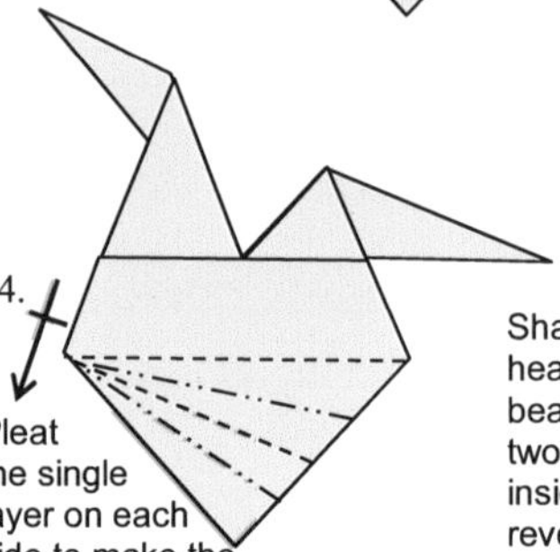

5\. Shape the head and beak with two small inside-reverse folds.

Draw some eyes if you want to.

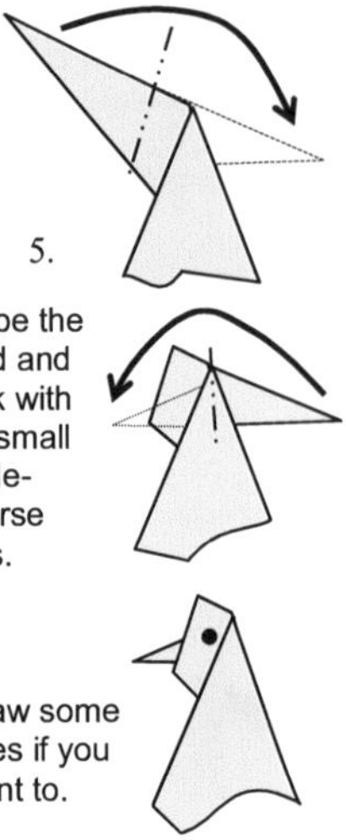

6\. Fold the point up to make a line, then cut it off !

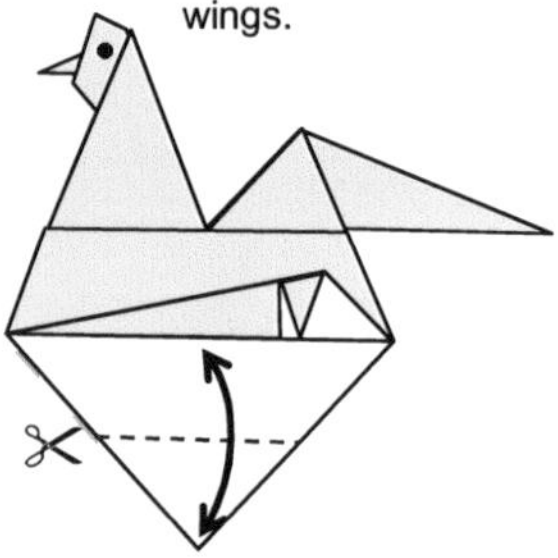

7\. Refold the cut-off part into a little Preliminary fold. This is the egg. …or is it the start of another tiny chicken? Oooh!

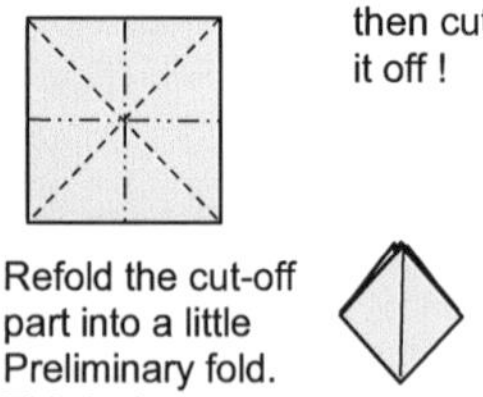

The egg slots into the back of the chicken. Ideally, the flaps on the egg go either side of the neck and the tail.

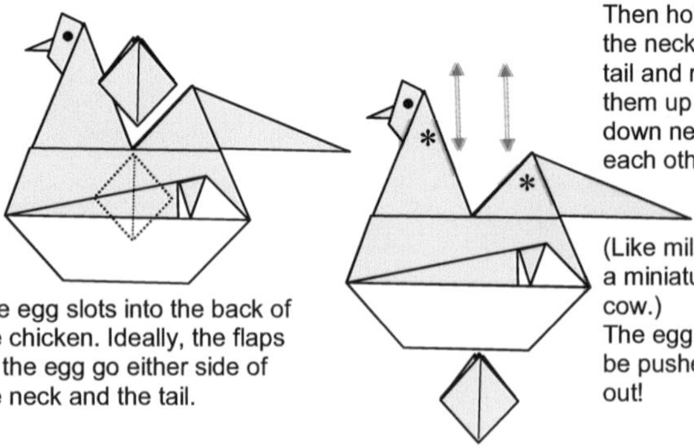

Then hold the neck and tail and rub them up and down next to each other.

(Like milking a miniature cow.) The egg will be pushed out!

It really is pushed out! Try it upside-down! Or take it into space and amuse astronauts!

Cat and Fox

Models inspired by many designers

1. Head.
Start with a Preliminary fold.
If you can, try to make it with only one diagonal fold so the face is smooth.

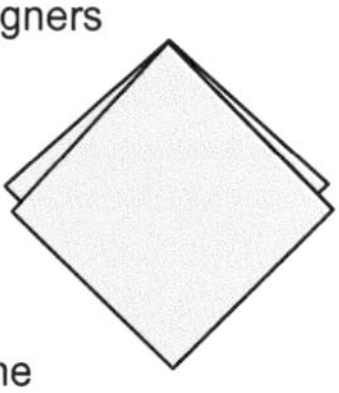

2.
Pull up the inside points (by reverse folds) to make the ears. Decide how big you want them to be.
A fox might have bigger ears than a cat, for example!

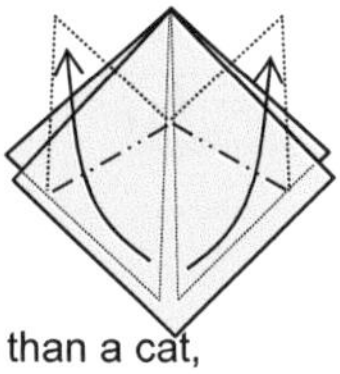

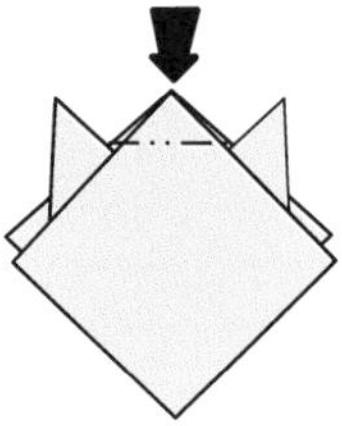

3.
Sink the top of the head. To do this move, crease it very sharply where shown, then unfold the model back to the square…

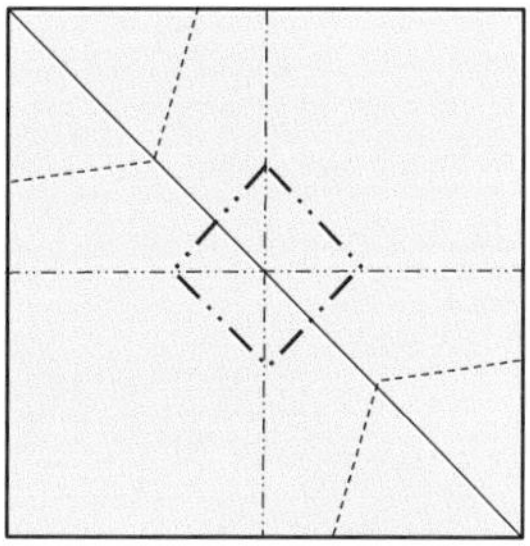

4.
Make the creases in the middle all into mountain folds by careful pinches, then re-assemble the model. This centre part should 'sink' into the head.
If this is too hard, just do a mountain-fold at step 3 instead.

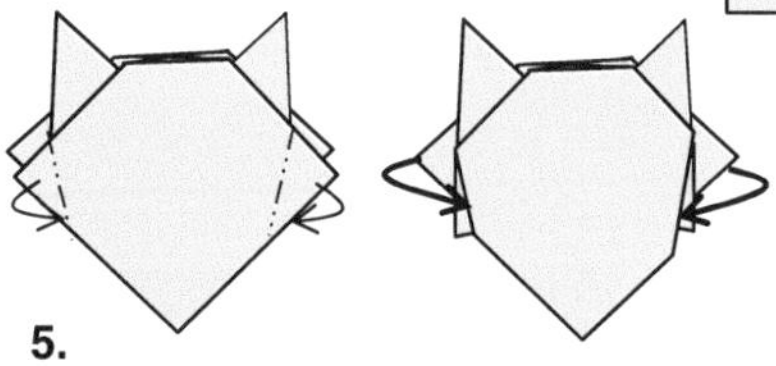

5.
Shape the sides of the head by inside-reverse folds on one side to make little pockets, then tuck the points on the other side into them to hold the head together.

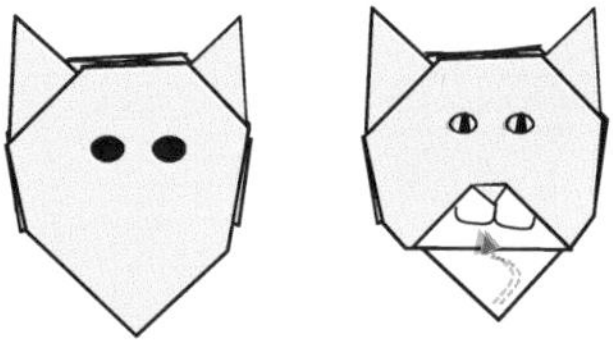

6.
For the fox, stop here. For the cat, shape the face and nose, similar to the puppy on page 5. You can also tuck the underneath point up inside the head.
Draw on eyes and mouth if you want.

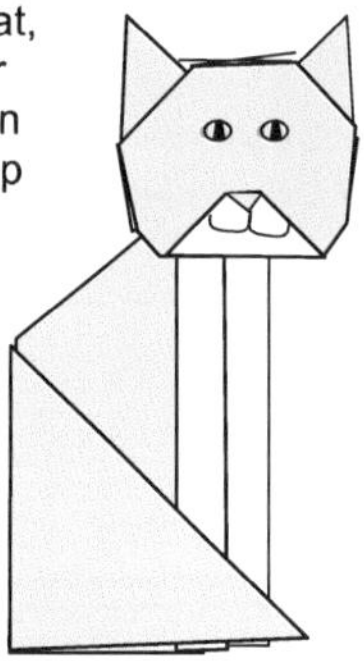

7. Body
Start with the first 4 steps of the Puppy body on page 5. You can make the front legs a little thinner than the puppy and make the tail go a little further across.
For the cat, stop here.
For the fox, make the rear end like the puppy, by pleating in and out, but try to give it a slightly larger tail if you can.

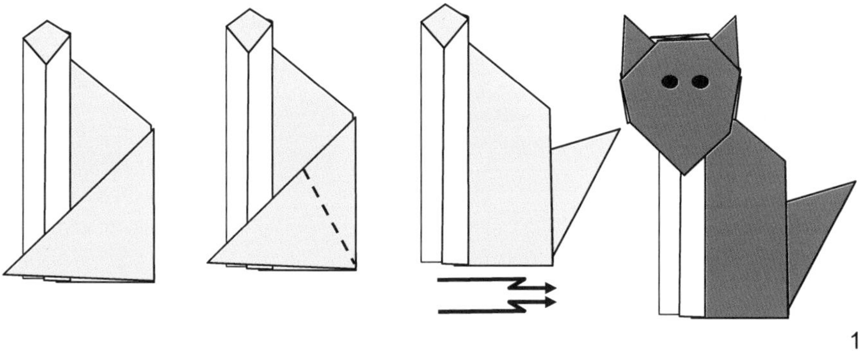

Fancy Box

Model by Dokuohtai Nakano

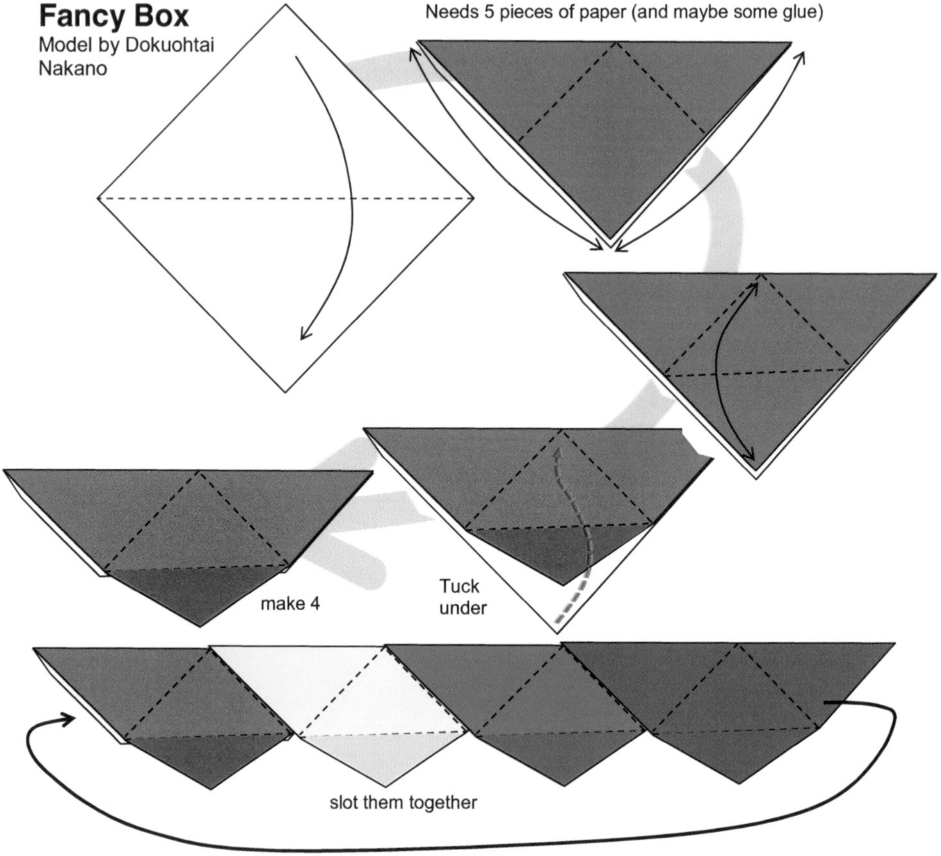

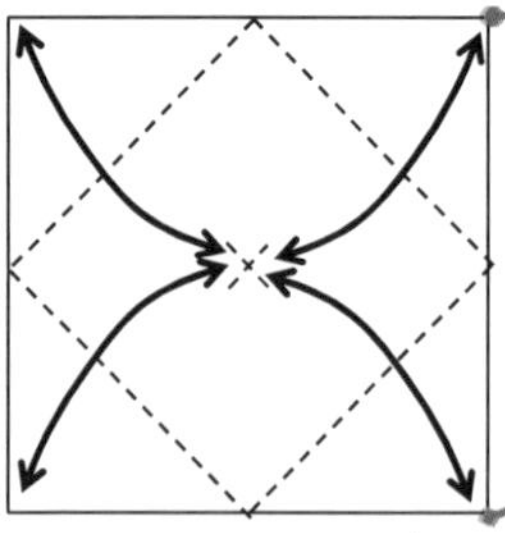

Find the middle of the 5th sheet (pencil and ruler, or make some small folds). Fold and unfold all the corners.

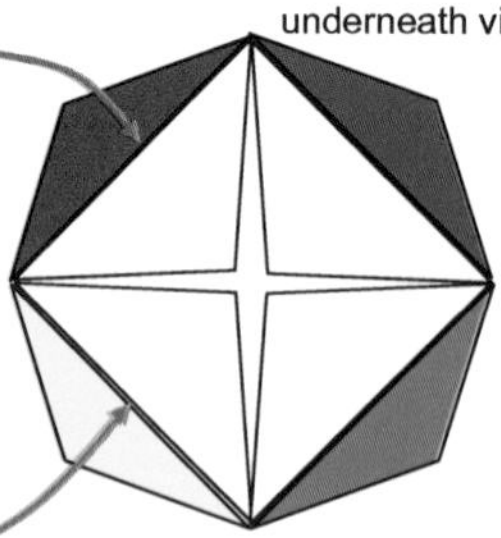

slot the triangles from the 5th sheet into the slits at the bottom of each module

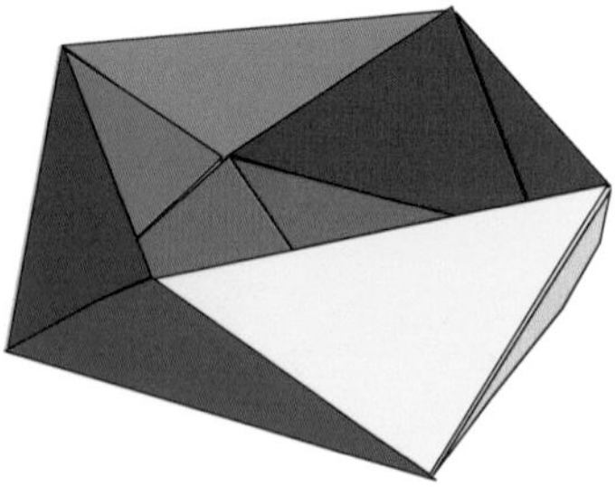

You can make it triangular too!

Jumping Frog Traditional model (but with a little twist from the author!)

1.

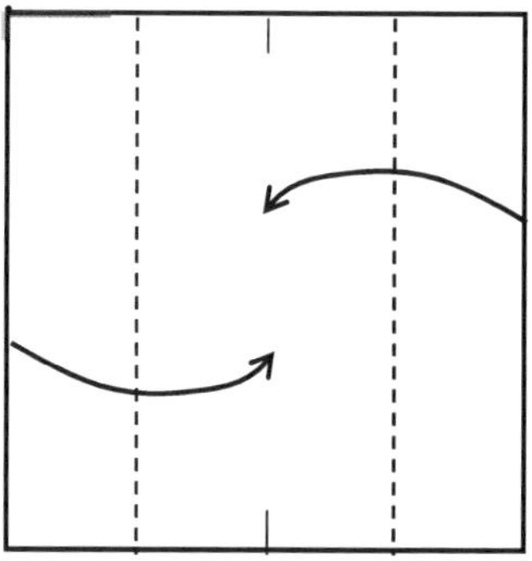

Make a pinch in the middle of the top and bottom edges. Then fold the sides to the pinches.

2.

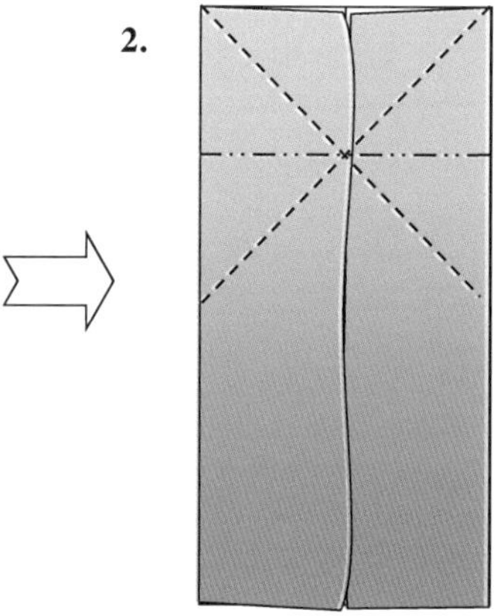

This is a little waterbomb base at the top end of the paper

3.

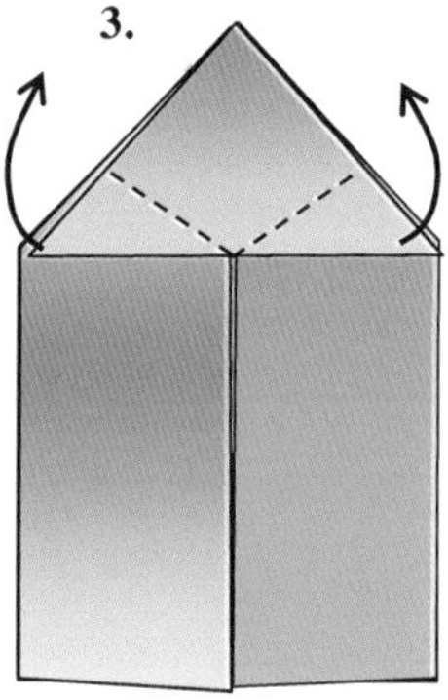

4.

5.

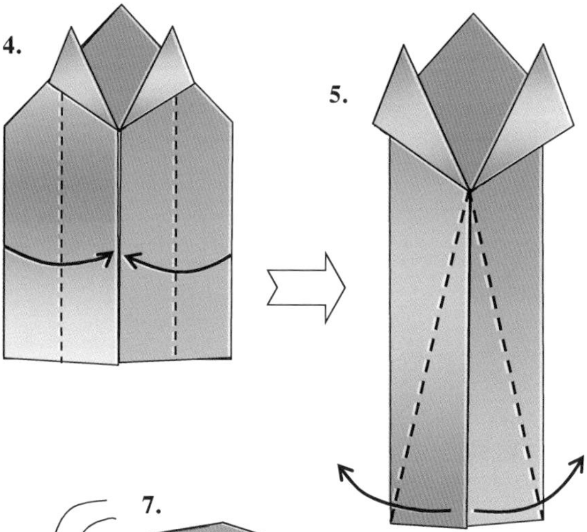

6.

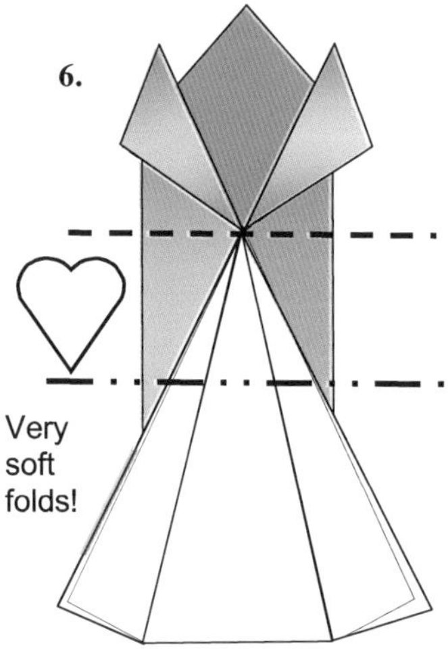

7.

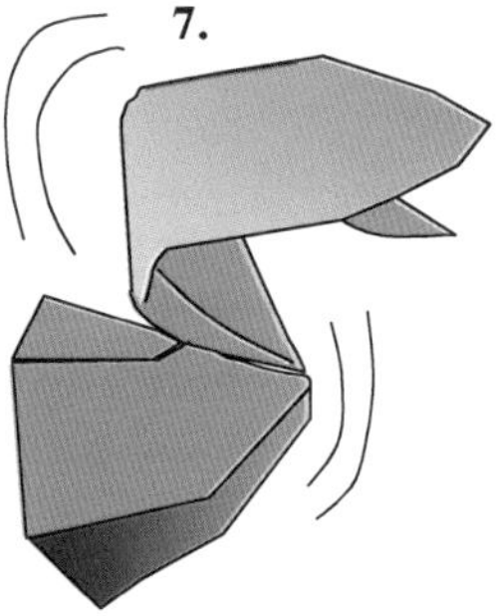

Gently squash and release to make it jump.
Or - hold it up to the light to see the back legs as it shines through. (That's my bit!)

You can start with a rectangle of thicker paper, or even a business card. Start from step 2.
Don't squash your frog too hard or it will die!

Tulip Flower Traditional model

Start with a waterbomb base (page 8, remember?)

1.

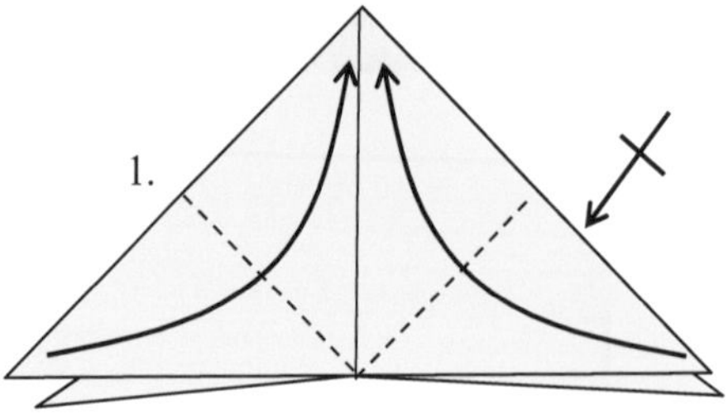

Fold the sharp corners up to the right-angle corner.
Note the "repeat behind" symbol to remind you to do it on the other side also.

2.

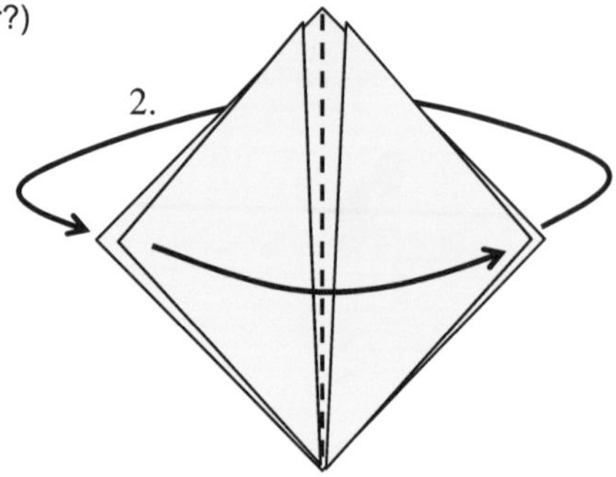

Now fold one of the sides over from left to right, like turning the pages of a book, and do the same on the other side. You end up with it smooth on both sides and the pointy parts are trapped inside.

3.

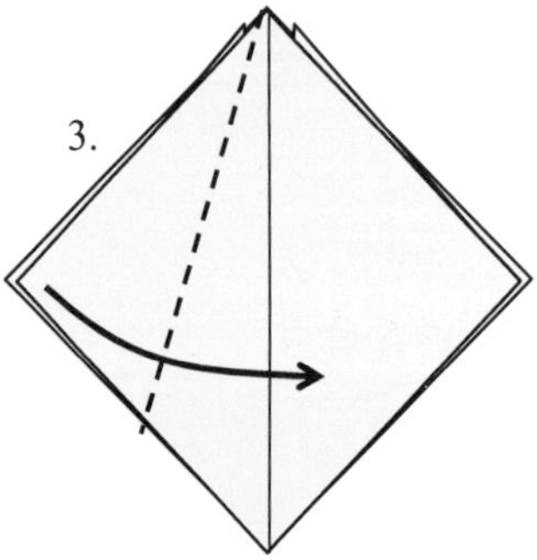

Make sure that you keep it the same way up.
The pointy parts are at the top.
Fold one edge **softly** about 2/3 of the way in

4.

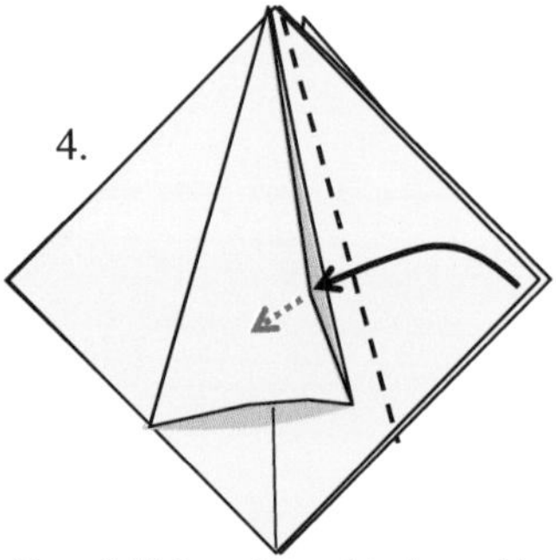

Now fold the other side in and try to tuck it into the slit along the side of the first one. It won't go in very far, and it won't lie flat, but try your best.

5.

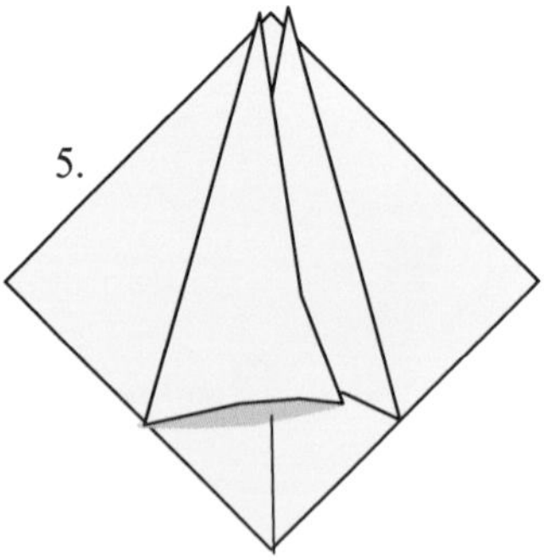

Repeat the last two moves on the other side

6.

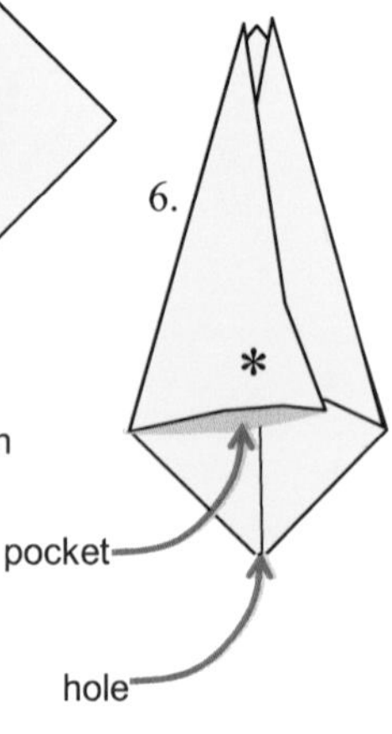

Place a finger inside the pocket and your thumb outside where shown (*) and hold tight while you blow hard into the hole at the bottom (hold on both sides – you need two hands!)

7.

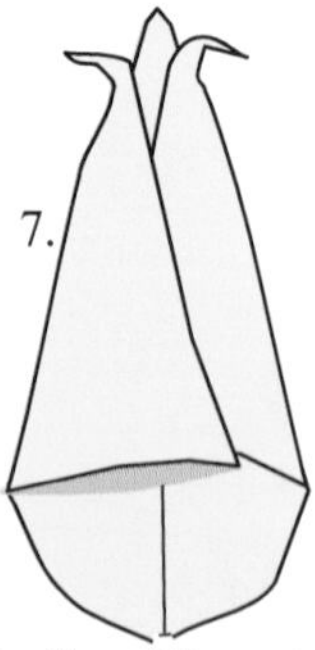

Curl the tips of the petals –maybe you can wrap them around a pencil

Tulip Stem

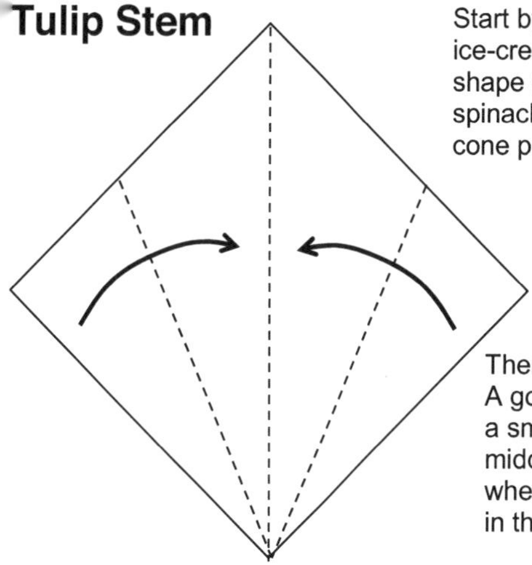

Start by folding an ice-cream cone shape (vanilla in a spinach flavour cone perhaps?)

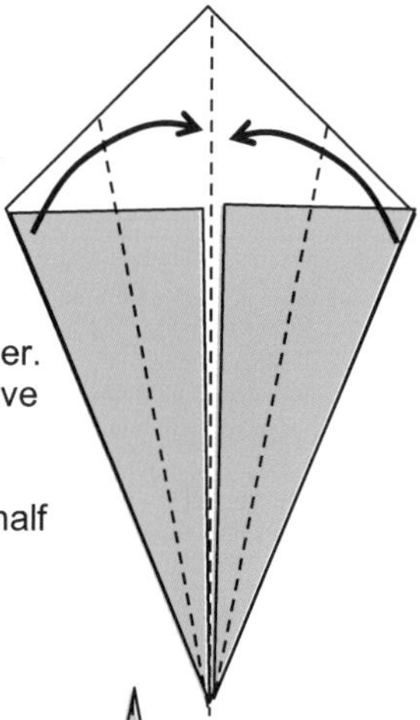

Then make it thinner. A good tip is to leave a small gap in the middle – it helps when we fold it in half in the final move.

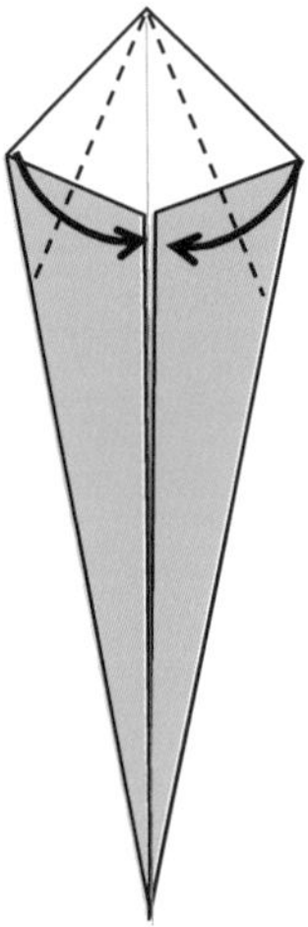

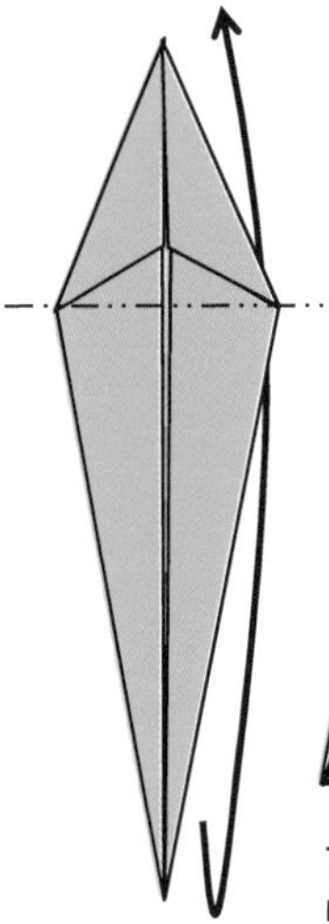

Mountain fold

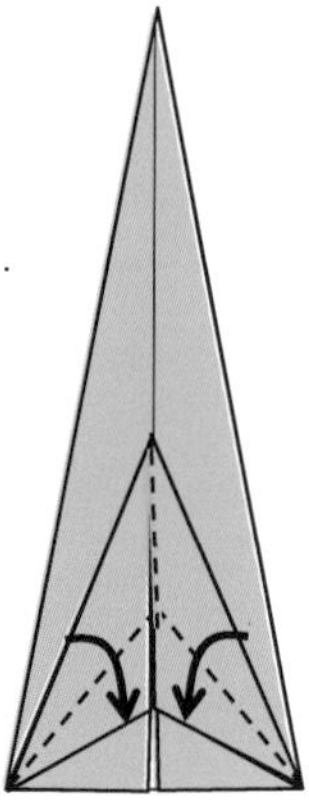

This is called a rabbit's ear fold. It makes the part stick up, rather like a rabbit's ear!

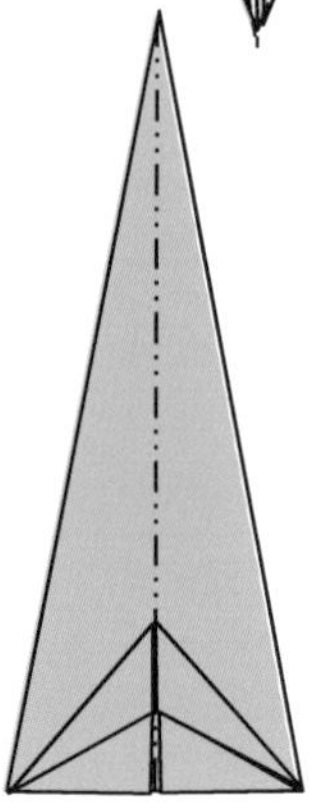

Finally, mountain-fold the whole stem in half along the mid-line, and place the tip into the hole at the bottom of the flower.

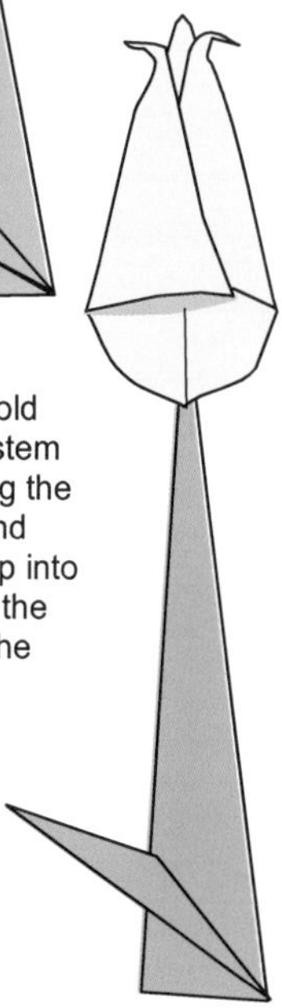

If you adjust the stem you should be able to get it to stand up.
(otherwise, Blu-tack is a wonderful invention!)

Heart

Model by
David Raynor≠

1.

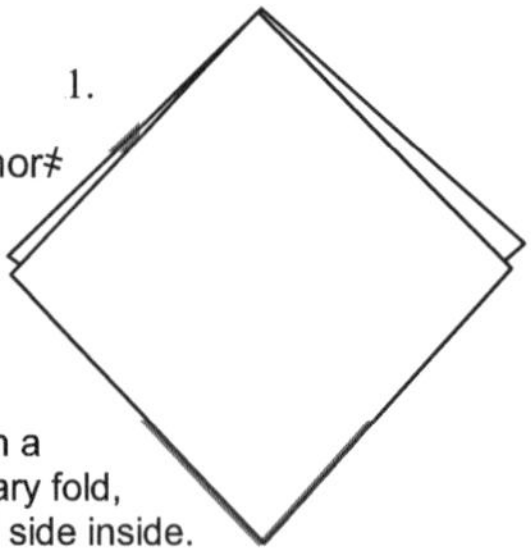

Start with a
Preliminary fold,
coloured side inside.
Open points are at the bottom.
If you can, try to make the Preliminary fold with only one diagonal fold, so the face is smooth.

2.

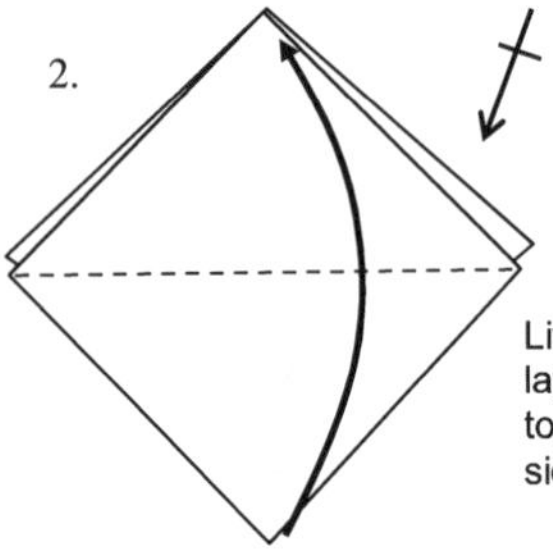

Lift the single layer up to the top, on both sides

3.

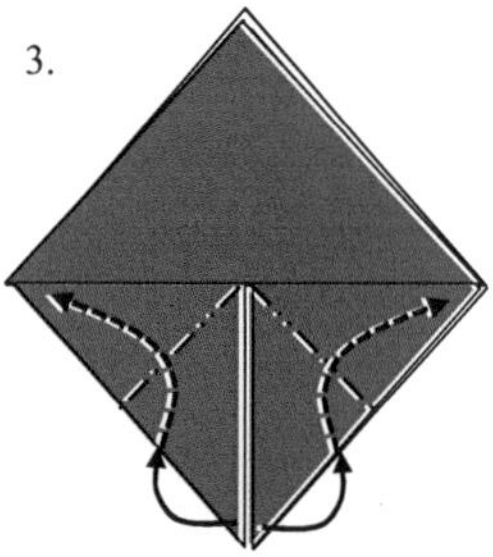

Inside-reverse folds

4.

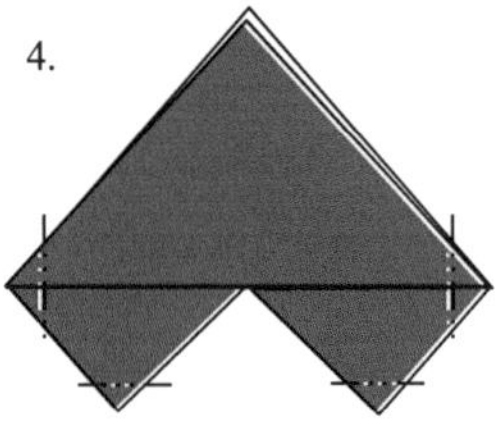

Fold the tips inside.
On both sides of the model*
and don't forget the points inside created by step 3.

5.

Result!

* Improvements can be made in step 4. Fold the tips on one side as inside-reverse folds. This makes little pockets. The tips on the other side can then be tucked into those pockets, holding the sides together.
It is similar to the cat's head on page 11.
It is also possible to round-off the corners even more, with extra, really tiny folds. It is fiddly, but worth it.

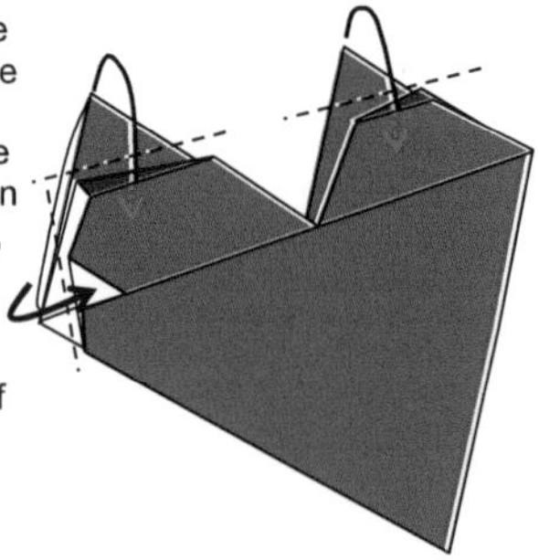

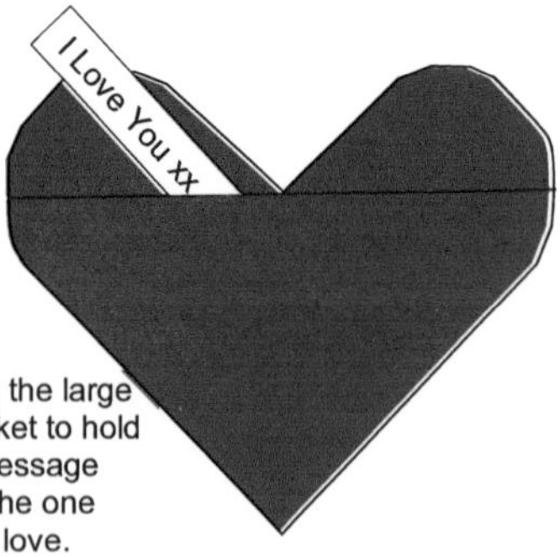

Use the large pocket to hold a message for the one you love.
Ahhh!

≠ - I'm not the only person to discover this model. If you play around with paper, I'm sure you will discover models too – they may have been already invented by someone else, but it doesn't make you any less creative!
This one was discovered by Michelle Tait in 1994, aged just six! (And probably by others also…)

Simple butterfly

By Dokuotei Nakano

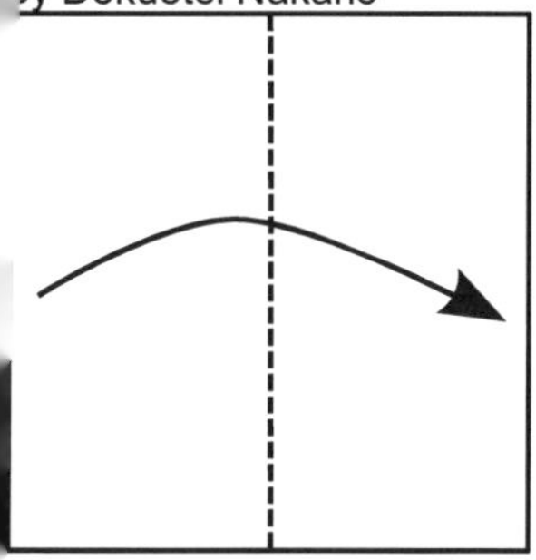

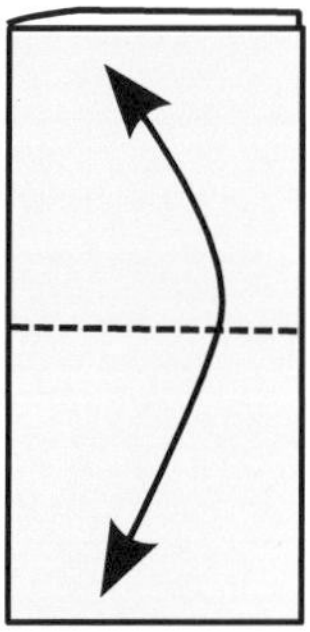

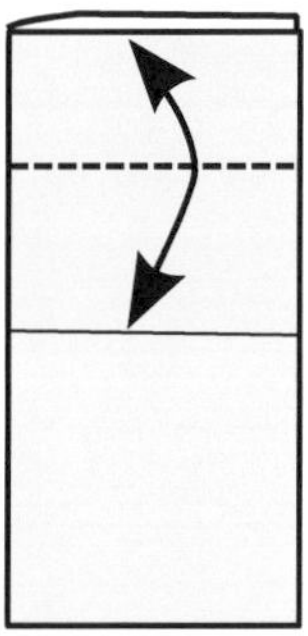

Soft fold, just to mark it

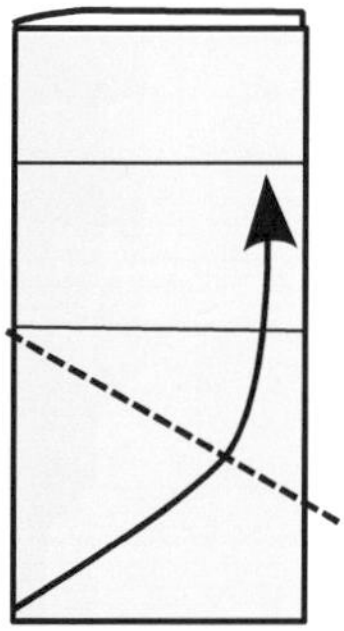

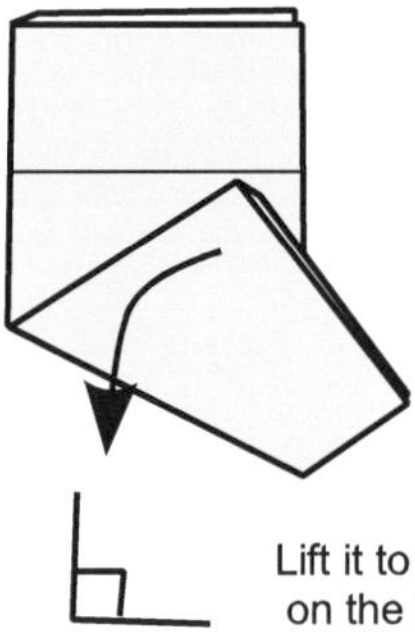

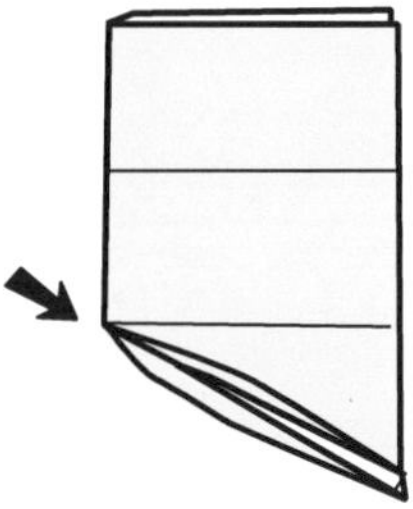

Lift it to vertical and then squash it by pressing on the folded edge

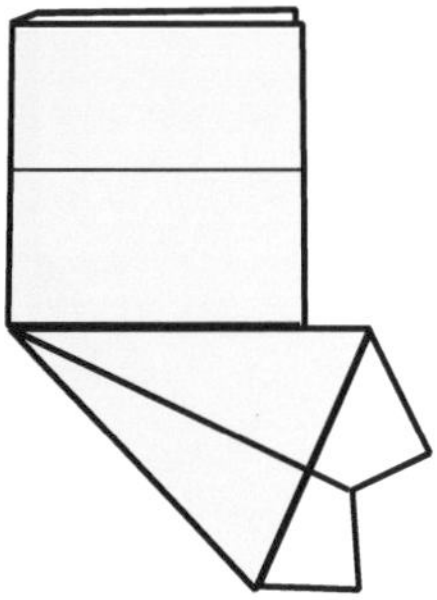

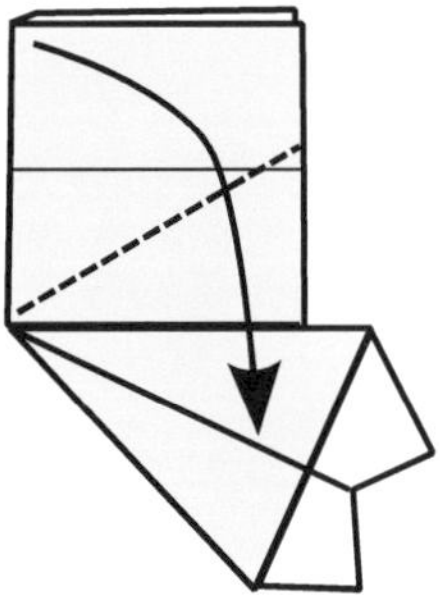

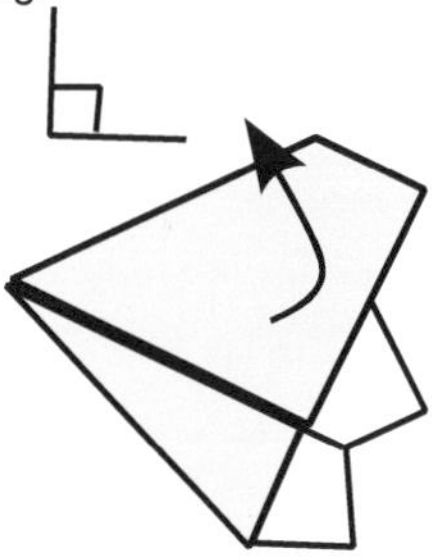

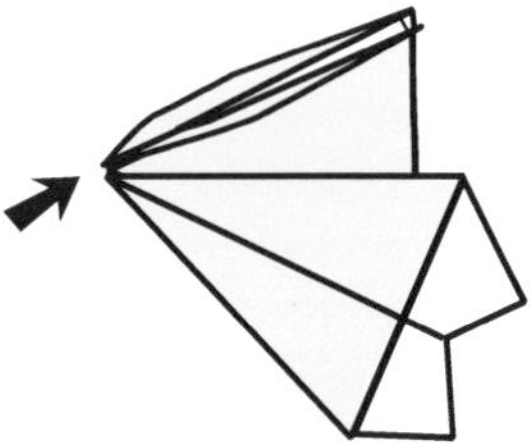

Lift to vertical and squash it.

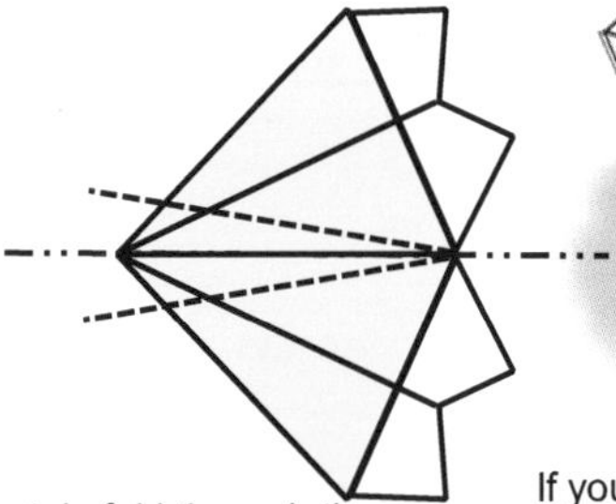

Mountain fold through the body, then valley fold the wings up on each side

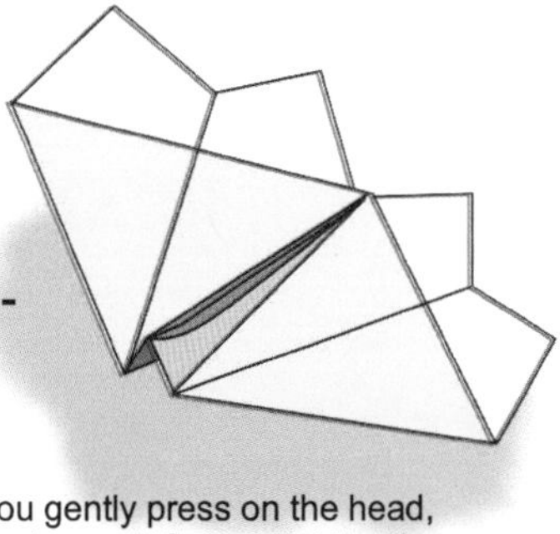

If you gently press on the head, the wings will flutter slightly, like when a butterfly is sunning itself.

Cup (it really holds water!)

Traditional model

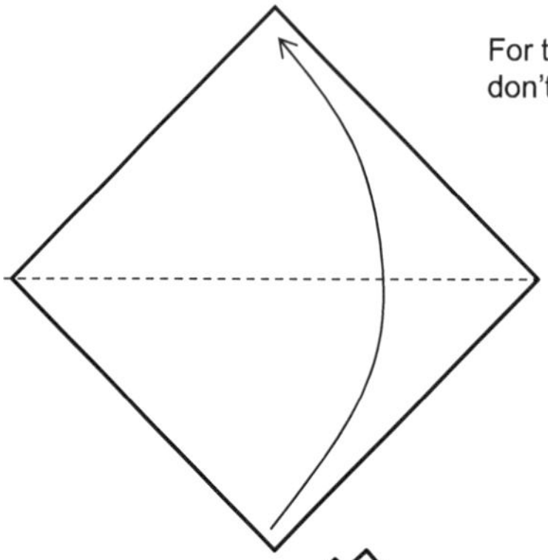

For the most water-proof results, don't make very sharp creases!

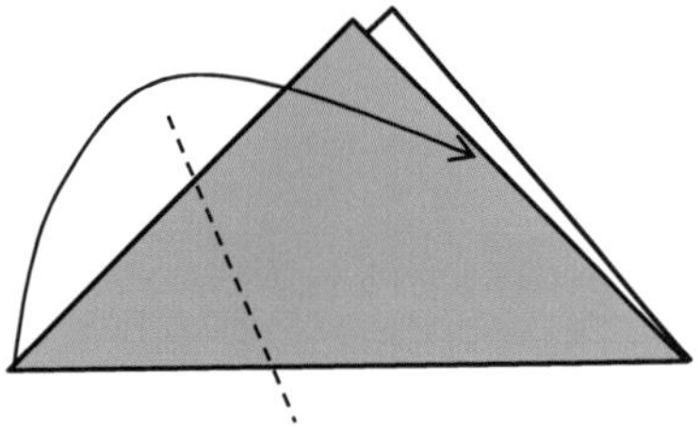

Fold one point across so that the top edge is parallel to the bottom folded edge.
Repeat with the other point.

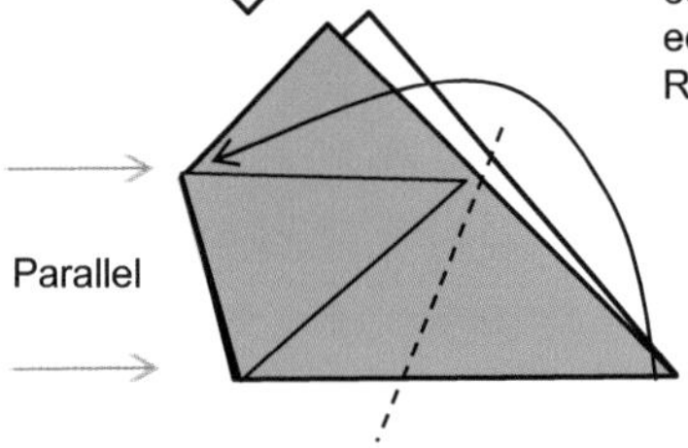

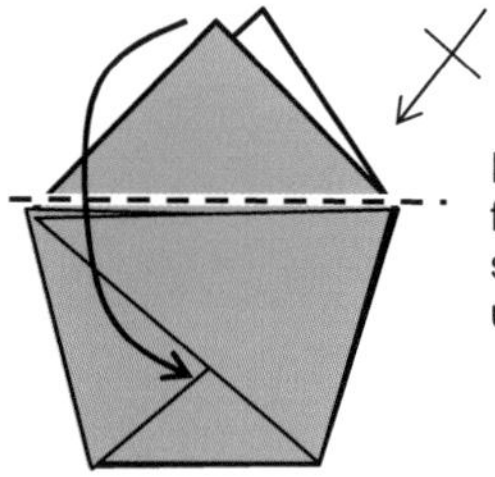

Fold the triangle flaps down on both sides, then open it up to make the cup

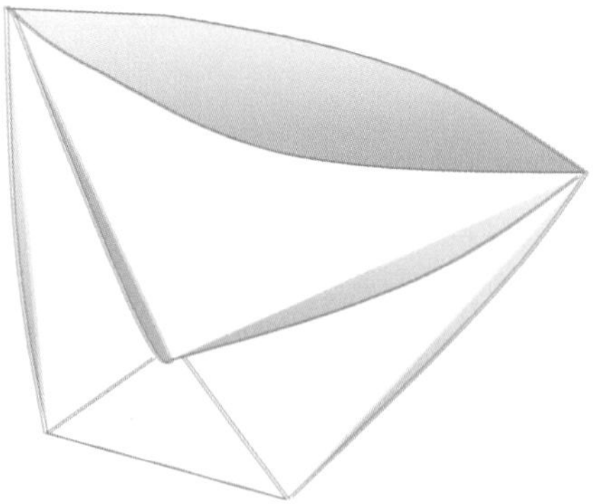

This fold is taught in the US Army Survival Manual.

If you make it out of strong paper (e.g. brown parcel paper) you can hang it up by string under the flaps each side and boil water over a camp stove! (Don't use synthetic string as it might melt.)

Or you can make a neat little package by folding both flaps to the front and tucking them into the triangular pocket.

Five-Pointed Star or Pentagon

Traditional model taught to Japanese children.

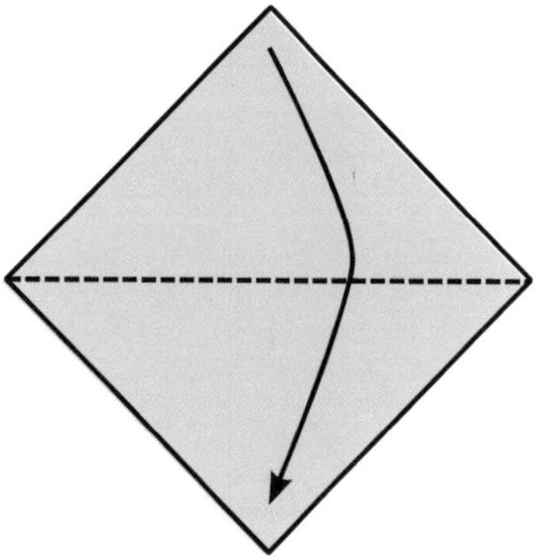

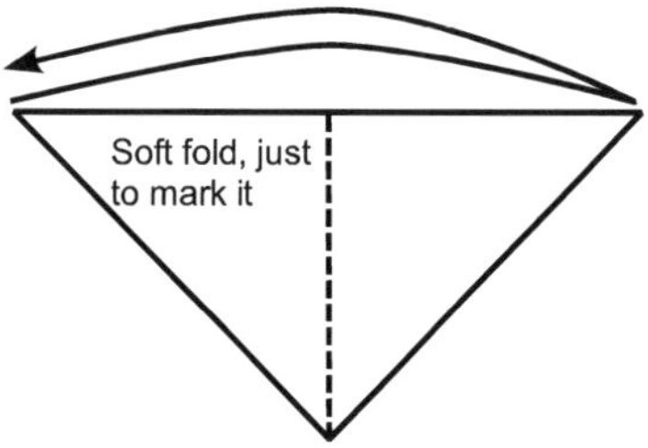

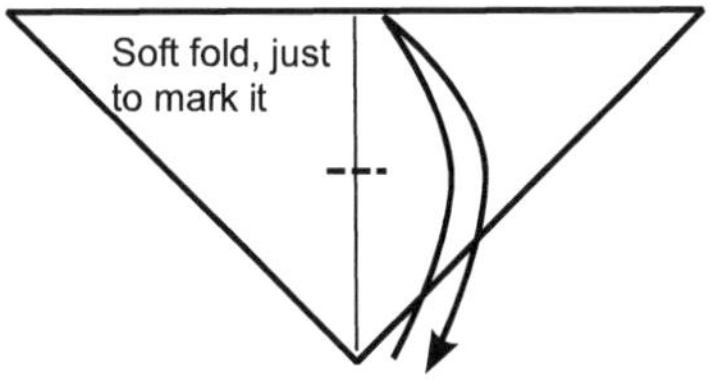

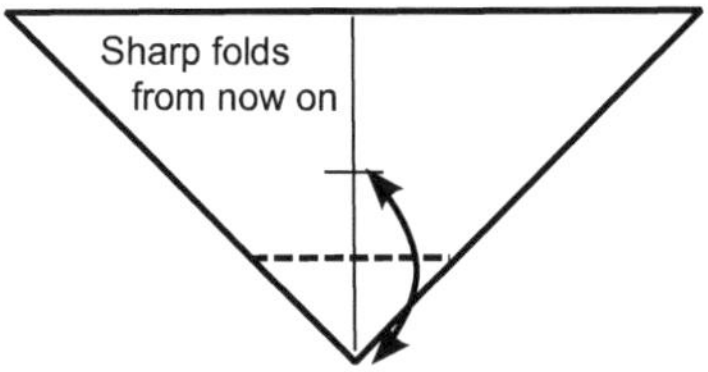

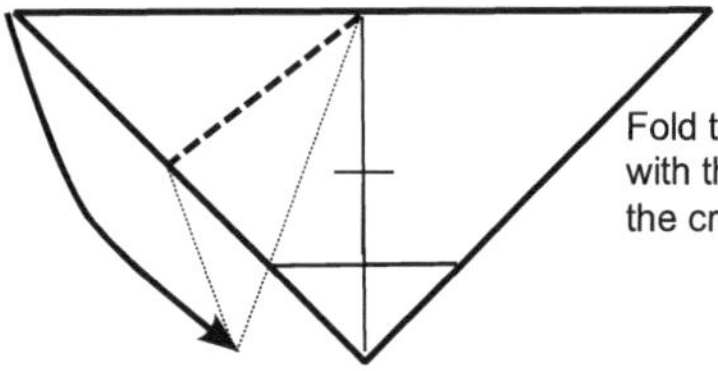

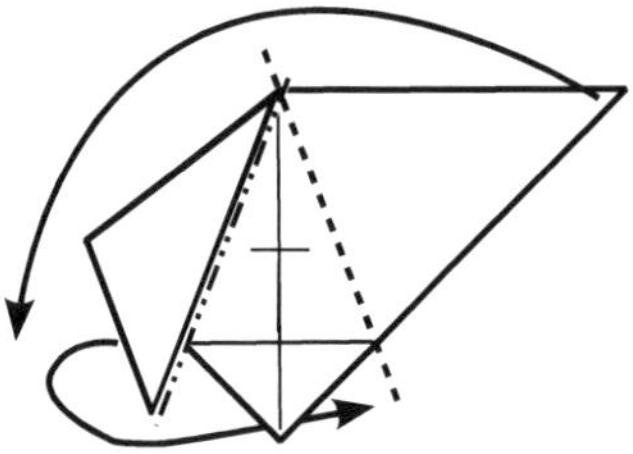

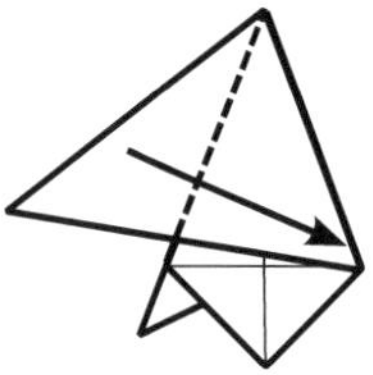

Mountain-fold the triangular flap behind, then fold the other corner along a line that ends at the crease

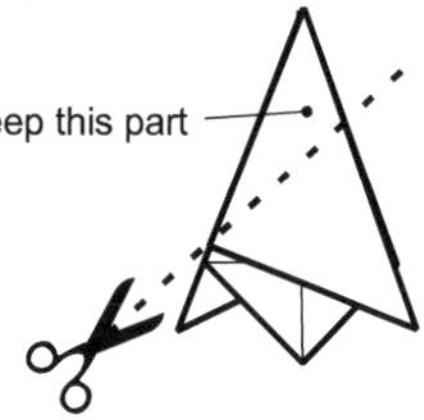

For a star, cut at a sharp angle

Unfold it

Adjust the folds if you want a 3-D effect

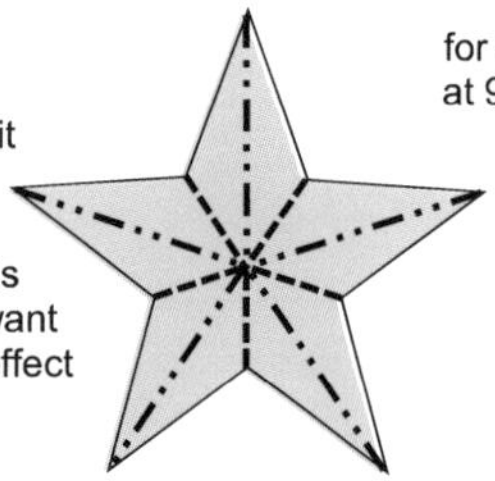

for a pentagon cut it at 90° to one edge

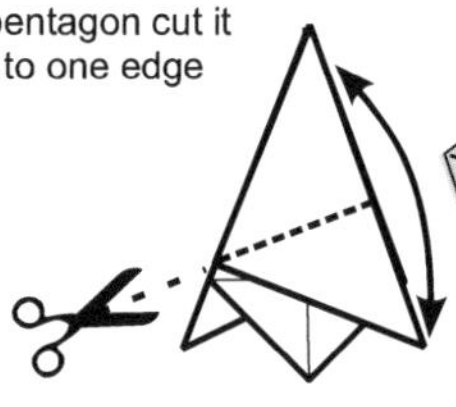

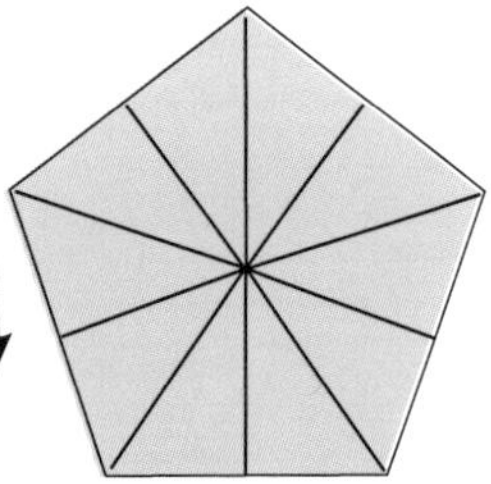

use it for flowers or other special models

The author learned this from a good book called “Origami Inspired by Japanese Prints” by Steve and Megumi Biddle.

Traditional simple box

This is known as a 'Masu' box - because it looks like an old wooden measuring cup used in Japan, called a masu

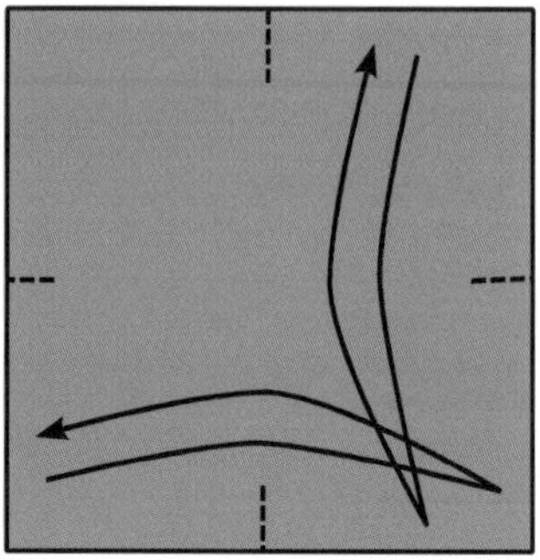

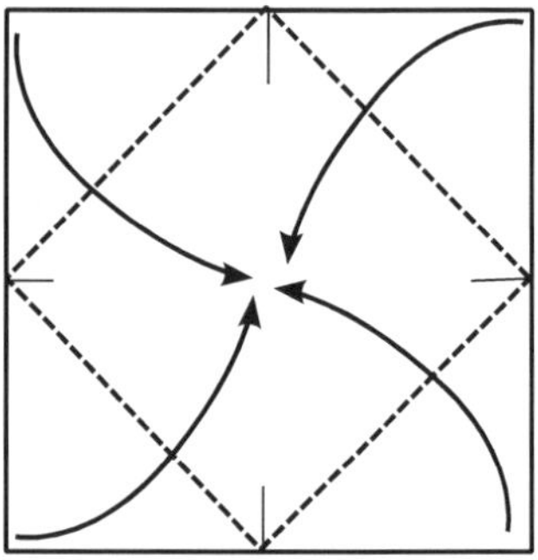

1.
Make a good pinch in the middle of each side, as a valley fold from the colour side. You could fold all the way acrosss, but that would put creases on the outside of the finished box.

2.
Fold all the corners into the middle. This origami move is called a 'blintz'.
Use the pinch marks as a guide, or use a ruler anc pencil to mark the centre.

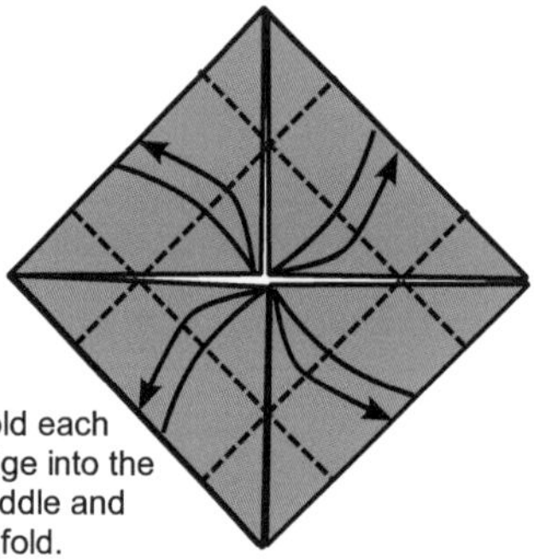

3.
Fold each edge into the middle and unfold.

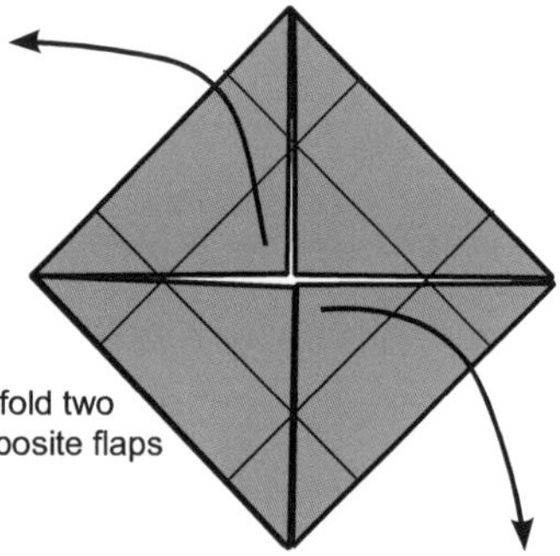

4.
Unfold two opposite flaps

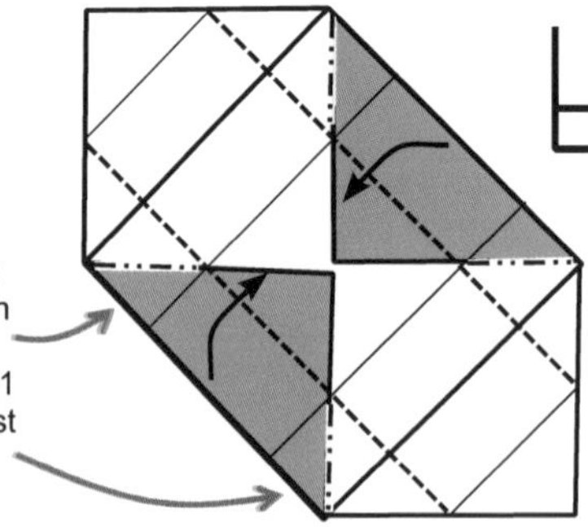

5.
Make mountain folds in these little squares (4 in total).
The pinches from step 1 will be here already, just extend them.

Then lift the sides up to the vertical position.

Traditional simple box - continued

6.
It should look a bit like this (maybe a bit wonkier, because the folds won't lie flat like my picture).

At one end, push in on those little diagonal folds and lift up the end as you do it.

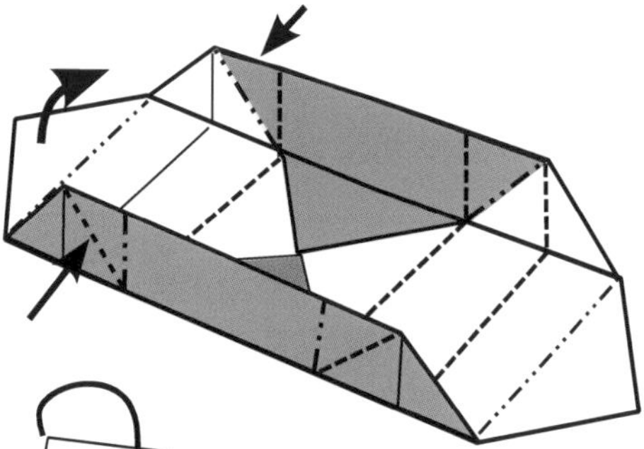

7.
Now fold the end over and into the box.

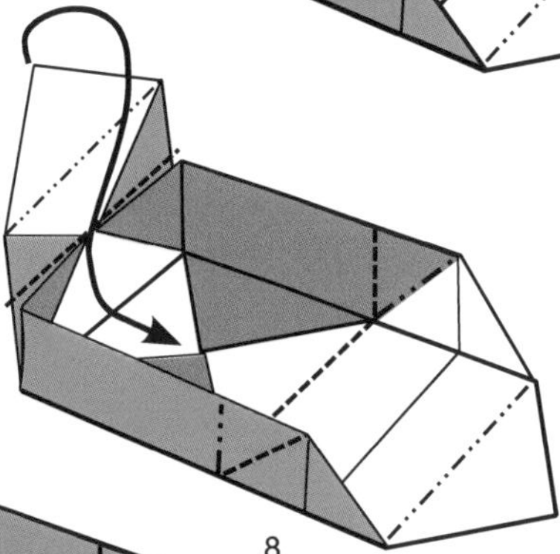

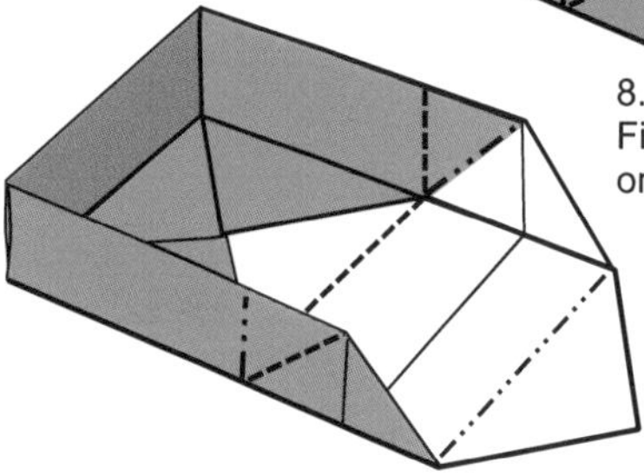

8.
Finally repeat steps 6 and 7 on the other end.

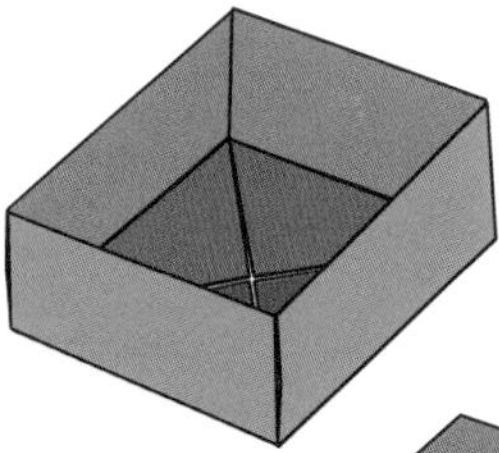

10.
If you want a lid, it needs to be a little bit bigger.
One way to do it, is to make another Masu, but at Step 3 don't fold the sides all the way to the middle.
You can use the first box to work out where the sides of the lid should be folded. Then carry on from there.

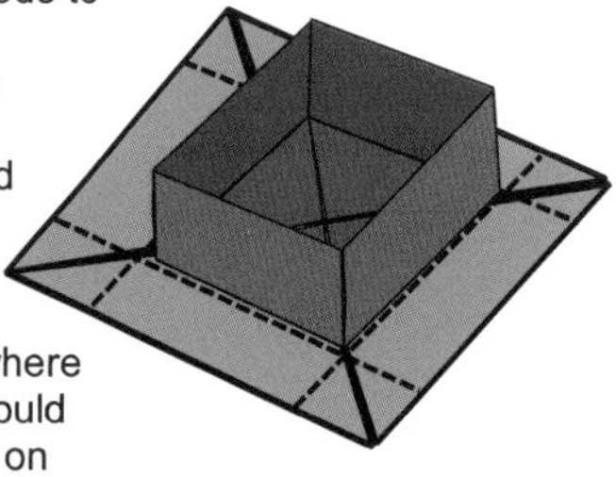

Well Done !

One real 'Masu' would hold enough rice for one person, for one day.

Boat

Traditional model

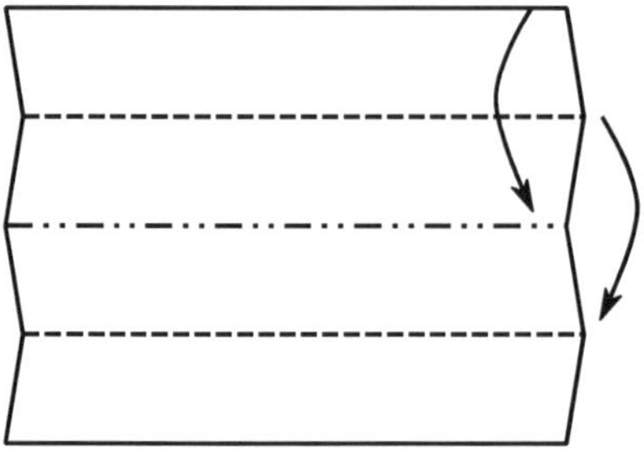

1:You can start with a square or a rectangle
It works well with either shape

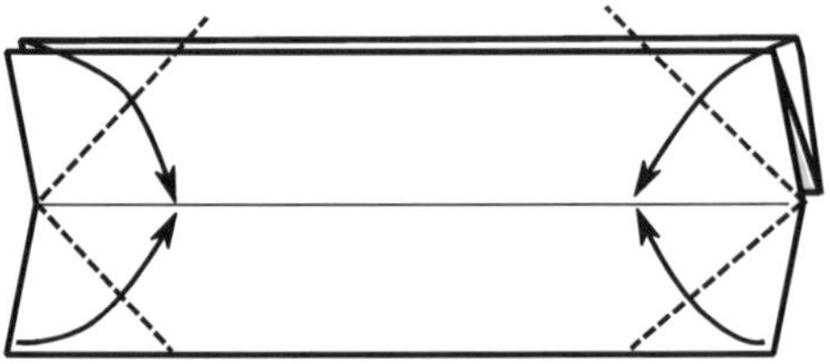

2: Put 3 layers one side, one layer on the other side.

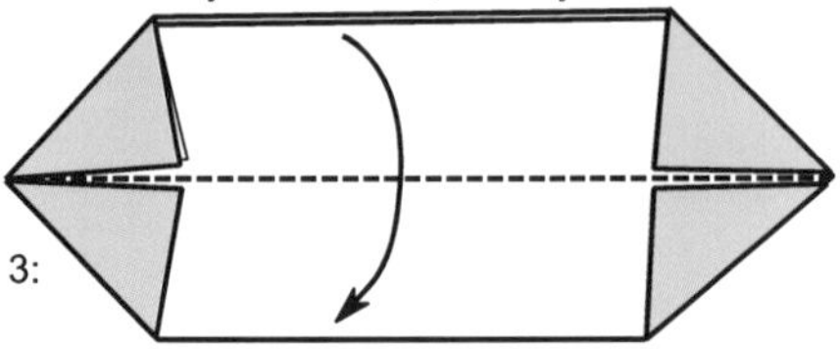

3:

4:
Spread apart
along the long side

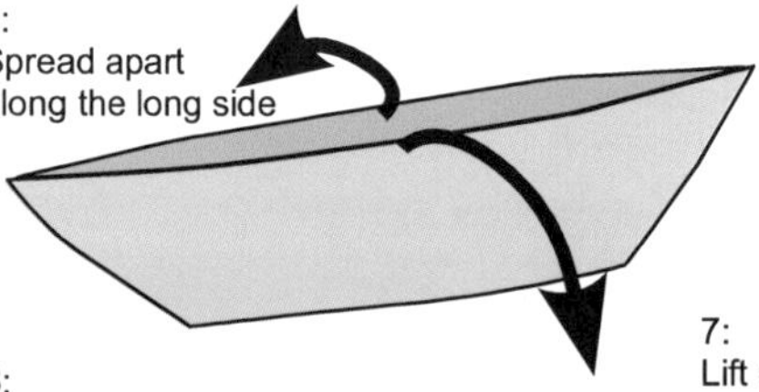

5:
The ends will lift up.
Squash them
down flat.

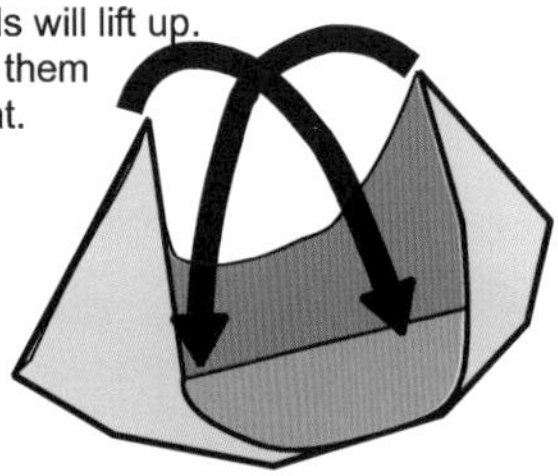

6:
You end up with a hexagon.
Mountainfold a small part at each end.

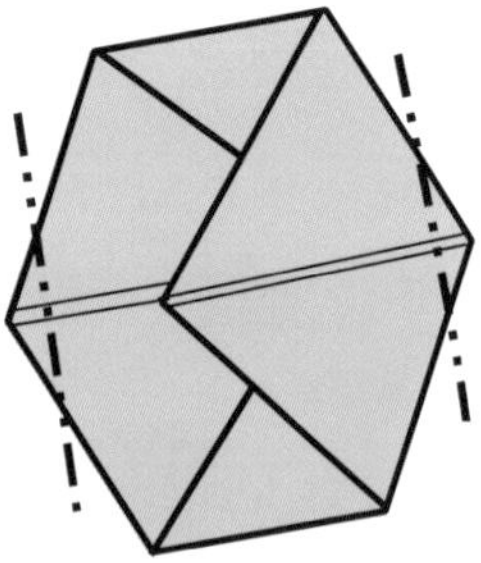

7:
Lift up the
ends again

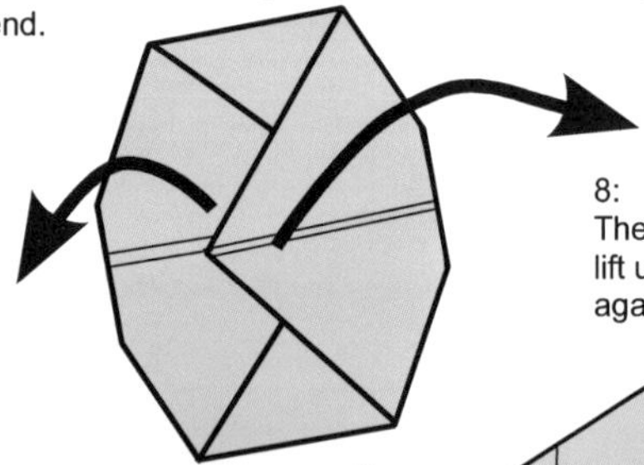

8:
The sides will
lift up
again.

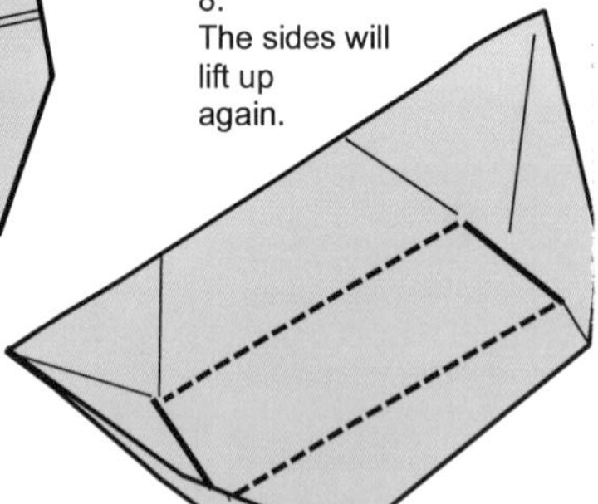

Firm up the creases in the bottom
so the sides will stay up.

It will float very well for a long time

Waterbomb

Traditional model

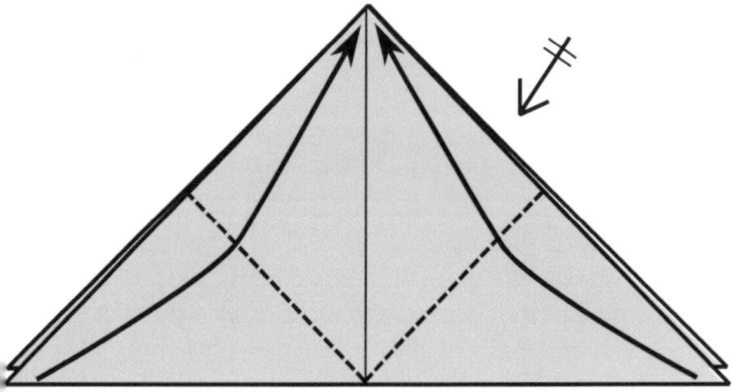

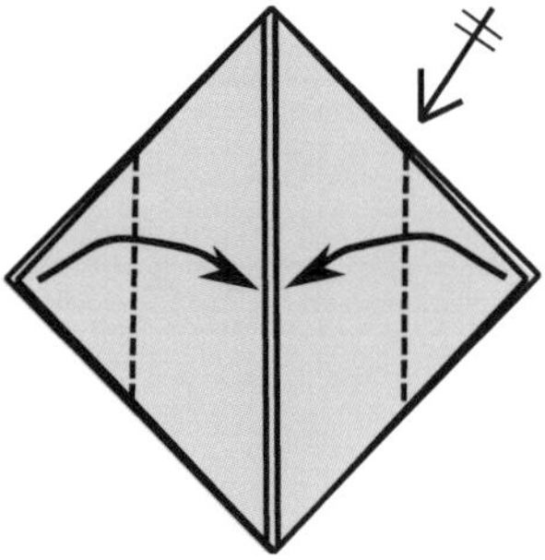

Start with the Waterbomb base
Fold up the corners on both sides.

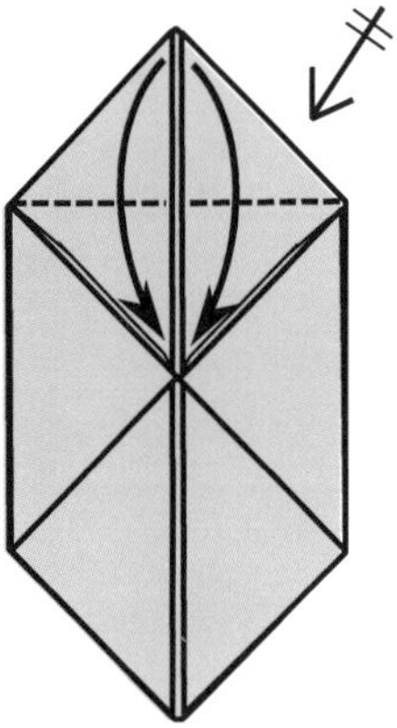

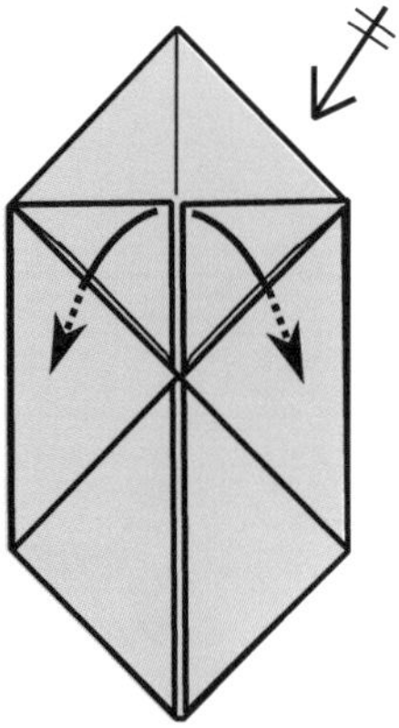

tuck the flaps into the pockets found at the top of the triangles, on both sides

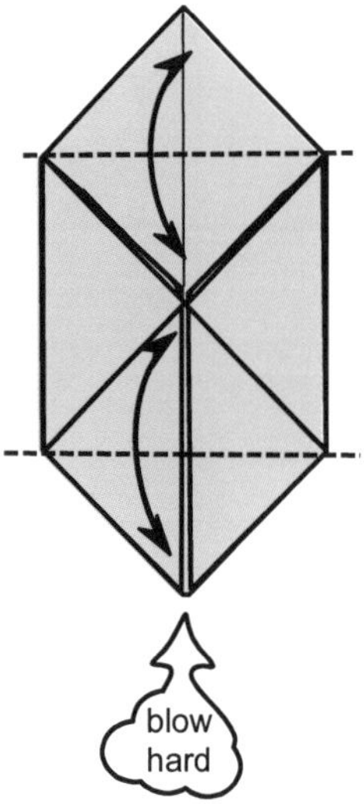

crease hard across the top and bottom, back and forth. Then blow very hard into the hole at the bottom

The traditional way to use it, is to fill it up with water through the hole, then throw it at your victim!
Or you can draw a small secret picture or a message in the middle of the square before you fold it, and look at it through the hole.
In some countries, children coax a fly to crawl through the hole and then they use it as a buzzer!

Harlequin cube

Variation of units created by Mitsunobu Sonobe

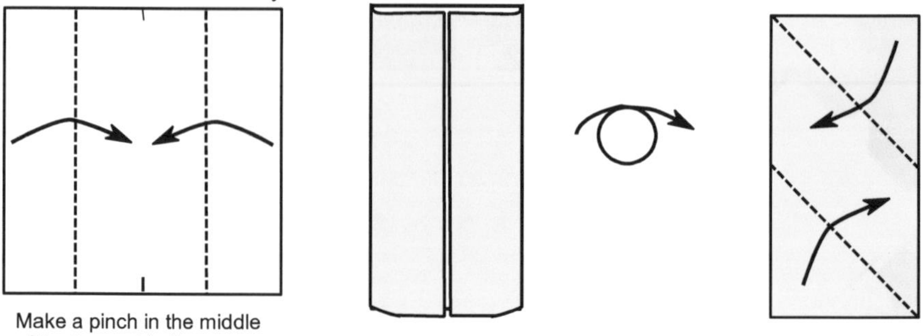

Make a pinch in the middle of the top and bottom edges, then fold the sides to meet it.

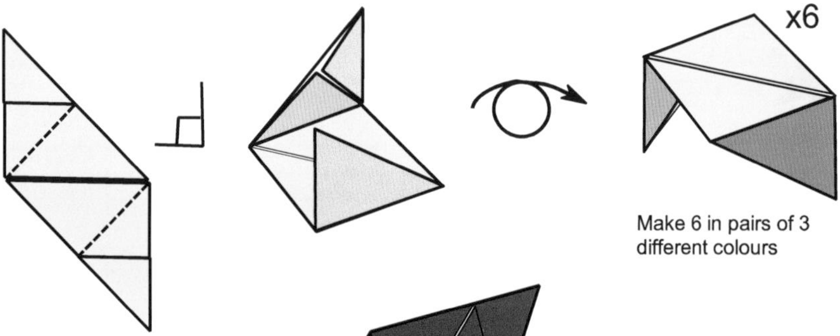

Make 6 in pairs of 3 different colours

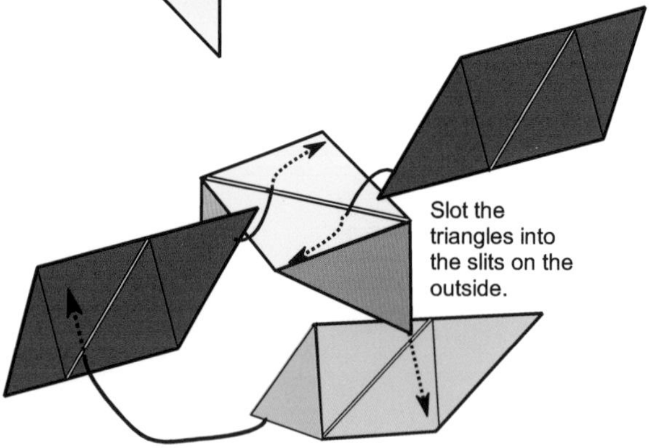

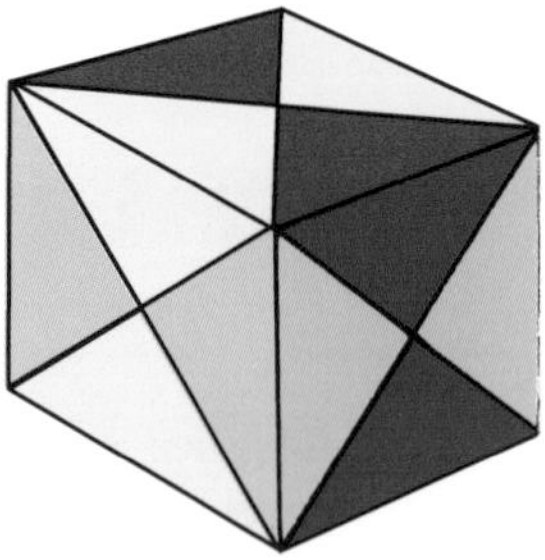

This is an example of 'modular origami'. Many spectacular shapes can be made from simple units like these. These units are inspired by ones called 'Sonobe units', named after their originator, Mitsunobu Sonobe. The ones here are simpler and are ok for this cube, but I can recommend that you look for Sonobe units in other publications if you want to make more complex shapes.

Perfect Paper Plane

Traditional model

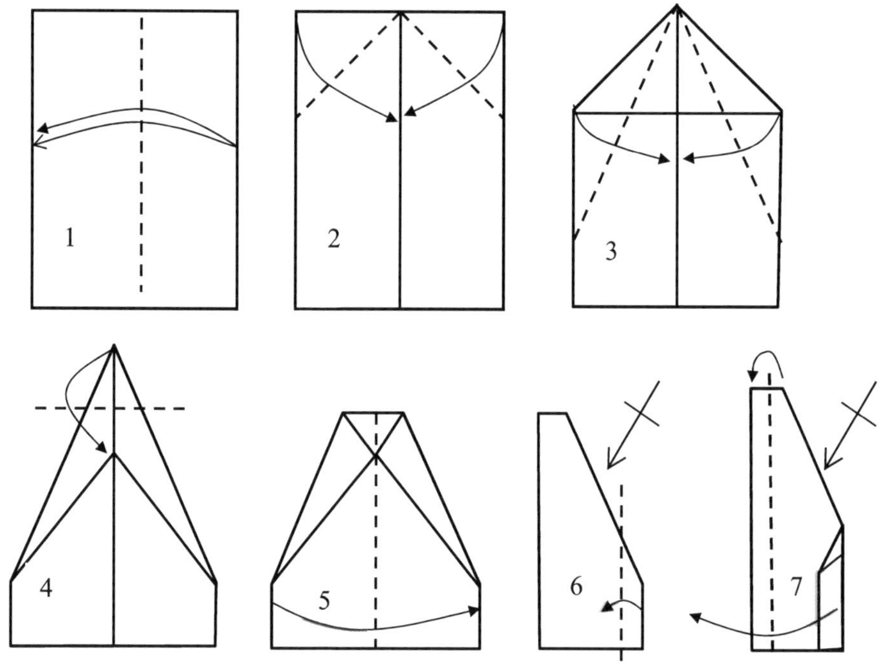

Just fold wingtip down by about 1cm and copy behind.

Now fold wing down by half the width of the nose and copy behind.

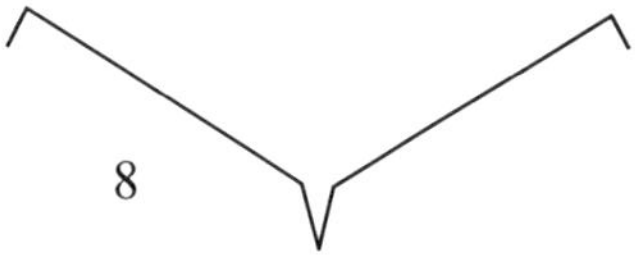

It is important that the folds in steps 6 and 7 are exactly parallel to the centre-fold. Step 7 is hard to do because the paper is so thick at the front.

Adjust the folds from steps 6 and 7 so that the model looks like this from the front – this slope is called *dihedral* and is important for good flight stability.
Note: it should look like this when it is flying, not when you are holding it . Try flattening out the folds from step 7 until it looks perfect.

Throw it smoothly, horizontally, not too fast. You are not trying to shot-putt!
With luck and good folding, it should glide serenely across the room

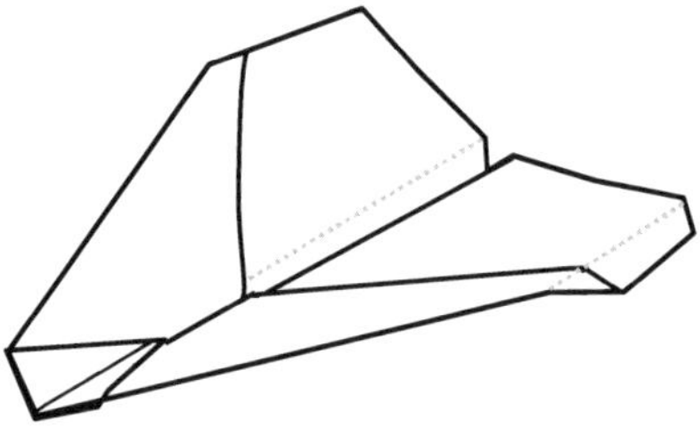

Simple talking frog

Model taught to the author by a child in 2004. It turns out to have been invented by Robert Neale, a creator well known in the Origami world. Look for his "Origami Plain and Simple", written in conjunctior with Tom Hull (a Mathematical origami expert himself) for some really good models.

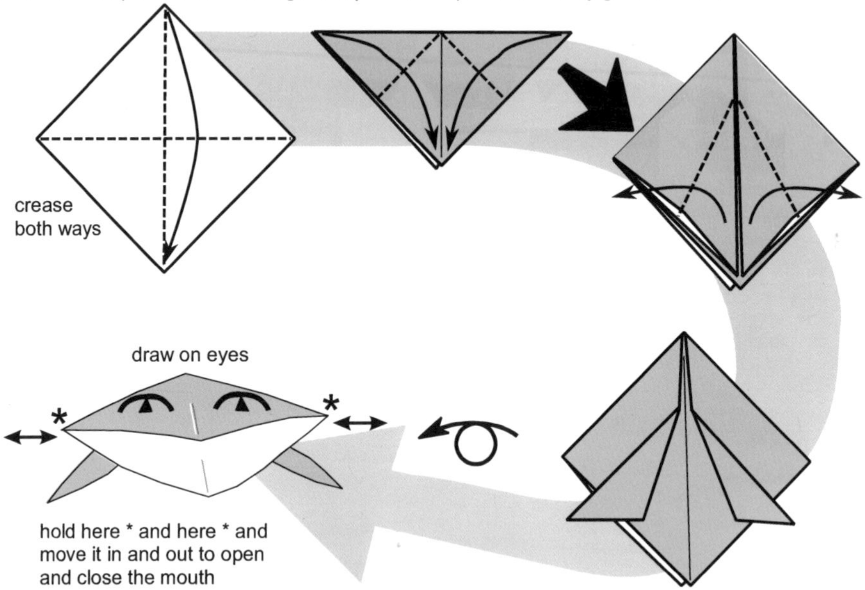

Penguin

Model by various creators

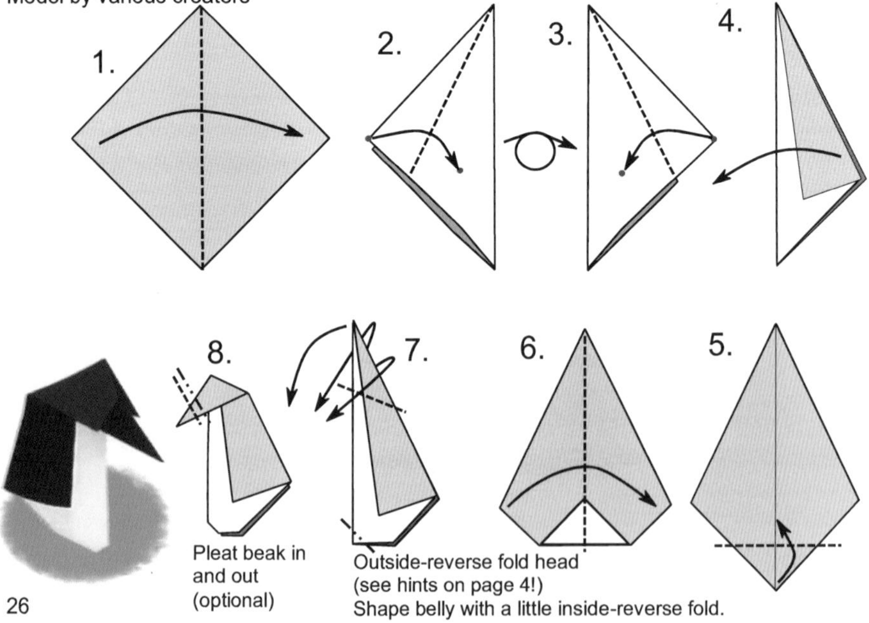

BOS Publications

1	History of Origami	John Smith
2	Origami and Mathematics	John Smith
3	History of Origami in Britain	David Lister
4	Origami Instruction Language	John Smith
5	Teaching Origami	John Smith
6	Geometric Division	Mick Guy
7	Chess Sets of Martin Wall, Max Hume & Neal Elias	Mick Guy & Dave Venables
8	Napkin Folds	John Cunliffe
9	Origami and Magic	Ray Bolt
10	Neal Elias: Selected Works 1964-1973	Dave Venables
11	Flexagons	Paul Jackson
12	Martin Wall: Early Works 1970-1979	Martin Wall

13	Orikata	John S Smith
14	Pureland Origami 1	John S Smith
15	Max Hume: Selected Works 1973- 1982	Dave Venables
16	18 of My Paperfolds	Paul Jackson
17	Origami Games	Mick Guy & Paul Jacksor
18	Philip Shen: Selected Geometric Paperfolds	Paul Jackson
19	Tony O'Hare: Selected Works 1973:1982	Daniel Mason
20	Origami Christmas Tree Decorations	Paul Jackson
21	The Silver Rectangle	John Cunliffe
22	In Praise of the Bird Base	John S Smith
23	Index: BOS Magazine 1-100	John Cunliffe
24	Index: BOS Magazine 101-120	John Cunliffe
25	Envelope and Letter Folds	John Cunliffe
26	Animal Origami	Edwin Corrie
27	Origami	Jeff Benyon
28	Structural Reconstruction	Ricky Wong
29	Pureland Origami 2	John S Smith
30	Paper People and Other Pointers	David Petty
31	Mor'igami	Jeff Benyon
32	Patterns in Paper	John S Smith
33	Animal Origami 2	Edwin Corrie
34	Neal Elias: Miscellaneous Folds I	Dave Venables
35	Neal Elias: Miscellaneous Folds II	Dave Venables
36	Neal Elias: Faces and Busts	Dave Venables
37	Jeffori 3	Jeff Benyon
38	Four 'igami	Jeff Benyon
39	Animal Origami 3	Edwin Corrie
40	Genius of Jan Willem Derksen	David Petty
41	Index: BOS Convention Packs	David Petty

2	Larry Hart: Selected Works (1971-1991)	Larry Hart
3	Pureland 3: Smith	John S Smith
4	Multi Plication	Jeff Benyon
45	The Origami of Stephen Palmer	David Petty
46	Modular Construction and Twists	David Petty
47	ABC of Origami	Eric Kenneway
48	Making Faces	David Petty
49	World of Fred Rohm I	Pete Ford
50	World of Fred Rohm II	Pete Ford
51	World of Fred Rohm III	Pete Ford
52	Origami Models Folded from Rectangles	John Morgam
53	Origami Models Folded from Silver Rectangles	John Morgam
54	More Origami Models Folded from Silver Rectangles	John Morgam
55	Sink or Swim with Ted Normington	Ted Normington
56	Petal Folds and More	Ted Normington
57	Pureland 4	John S Smith
58	Owrigami	Francis Ow
59	10 Pop-Ups	John S Smith
60	A Medieval Court in Origami	Julia Pálffy
61	Decorative Boxes from Single Squares	Arnold Tubis & Leon Brown
62	Animals and Birds	Tony O'Hare
63	Ship-shape and Bristol Fashion	Tony O'Hare
64	Faces'n'Fings	Tony O'Hare
65	Planar Modulars (CDRom)	David Petty
66	The Nativity - An Origami Scene	Lore Schirokauer
67	Selected Works of Quentin Trollip	Quentin Trollip
68	Which Came First ?	Bob Neale
69	3D Masks and Busts	Eric Joisel
70	Phillip Shen: More Geometric Paperfolds	Boaz Shuval

71	Origami Construction	Giles Towning
72	Darwinism	Ted Darwin
73	Max Hulme: A Second Selection	Max Hulme
74	Origami Under Construction	Giles Towning
75	Simple Origami	Penny Groom
76	Origami Constructed	Giles Towning
77	Don't Fold Under Pressure!	David Raynor
92	My Fundamentals	Kuni Kasahara

Occasional Booklets

Paperplay	John S Smith
Bibliography: Origami in Education and Therapy	John S Smith
COET	Editor: John S Smith

Other Booklets

Fold with Feeling	Nick Robinson
Hearts 3D	David Petty
Origami Favourites	Edwin Corrie

For information about;

Buying BOS Publications	*e-mail* supplies@britishorigami.info
Joining BOS	*e-mail* membership@britishorigami.info
Origami in General	*e-mail* secretary@britishorigami.info
Submitting material for publication	*e-mail* publications@britishorigami.info
Origami Teachers or Commissions	*e-mail* teachers@britishorigami.info
Please visit our website	www.britishorigami.info

Printed in Great Britain
by Amazon

24022589R00018